From Th
Mental

Edna Hunneysett

chipmunkapublishing
the mental health publisher

Published by

Chipmunkapublishing

PO Box 6872

Brentwood

Essex CM13 1ZT

United Kingdom

http://www.chipmunkapublishing.com

ISBN   ISBN 978-1-84991-696-7

Chipmunkapublishing gratefully acknowledge the support of Arts Council England.

Foreword

This book provides a valuable insight into the lives of those who live with difficulties in mental health and those who care for them. Its approach provides people with a voice - an opportunity to share with others the difficulties, challenges and joys that they face on the journey to recovery.

Its publication is timely, coming at a time when there is an increasing interest in mental health issues across England & Wales, and we must be grateful to Edna Hunneysett for her commitment to the sphere of mental health and for all the work that has gone into this book.

We journey towards a time when issues of mental health are better understood and I commend this book as a welcome contribution to that journey.

Richard Moth
October 2011

Rt Rev. Richard Moth, Bishop of the Forces, is the lead Bishop for the short term Mental Health Project 2010 - 2012 that the Catholic Bishops' Conference of England and Wales has established to further encourage and inspire us as communities of understanding.

About The Author

Edna Mary Hunneysett was born in 1940 near Stratford-upon-Avon, but in her infancy the family returned to a small rented hillside farm on the North Yorkshire Moors where she spent her childhood with six siblings. After passing her eleven plus examination, she attended a convent boarding grammar school for six years. She married in 1961 and years later, after having eight children, she began her academic career. She graduated with a BA (Hons) in Divinity in 1995 and gained an MA with distinction in 1998. Edna continued studying part-time for a further six years, researching attitudes towards people with mental illnesses with specific reference to Christian congregations under the tutorship of the Principal (now retired) of St. John's College, University of Durham.

Over recent years Edna has spoken in many churches and other venues, locally and nationally, raising awareness on the need of support for families where a member has a mental illness. As well as hands-on involvement with her family, now including eighteen grandchildren and one great grandchild, she locally facilitates monthly pastoral support groups, one for carers of people with mental illnesses and the other for people in the community who have a mental illness.

Edna lives with her husband in Middlesbrough and is a minister of the Word and of the Eucharist in her parish.

Previous publications (reviews at end of this book)

Our Suicidal Teenagers: Where are you God? (2009)
Chipmunkapublishing
(previously published as *Carers in the Community: Why have you forsaken me?*).

Pastoral Care Mental Health (2009)
Chipmunkapublishing

Acknowledgements

I am very grateful to all the very special persons who have contributed to the content of this book. It is only through their effort and time, often writing under difficult circumstances but with courage and tenacity, that it has been possible to have this book produced. I hope and pray that through their openness, firstly, that others will have more understanding of what life is like when a person has a mental illness and secondly, that as a consequence, there will be more support and pastoral care for them and for their carers.

Thanks to Grace Neal (www.foliofruit.com) for her illustrations:
Shine Your Light of Hope and Love
My Precious Lord
Jesus Crowned with Thorns

Thanks to Rt Rev. Bishop Moth, Rev. Professor John Swinton, and Brian Dowd for their input and support.

The front cover illustration is designed by our daughter Elizabeth, who produced this drawing when aged fourteen and in a severe clinical depression: From the heart, the fire symbolising the searing pain of suffering revealed through tears. A very special thanks to you Elizabeth because as a consequence of our journey together when you were so ill, my life took a different route and subsequently has been enriched by many, many individuals who have shared their stories with me.

I am grateful to Aleks Lech for painstakingly proof reading my book on behalf of Chipmunkapublishing.

From The Heart

Prologue

Stories are important. In a real sense we only know who we are because of the stories that we tell about one another and the stories that are told about us by others. When we want to communicate who we are, we tell stories about ourselves. When we try to describe other people, we tell stories about them. Stories provide the fabric that shapes who we are and how we see the world.

But what kind of stories do we tell about mental illness? The sad truth is that the stories we choose to tell about mental illness are often tragic, bizarre, frightening and sometimes quite dehumanising. Above all else, very often they are untrue. Normally when someone tells a story that is untrue about us, we simply tell a counter-story that corrects the untruth. But if we have a diagnosis of mental illness, people are much less likely to listen to our counter-story. So we end up being defined by other people's stories and this is a very risky place to be.

Edna Hunneysett wants to change that. She wants us all to hear the stories of people with mental illness and to allow these stories to change us. In this book she has gathered together a new set of stories about mental illness; a set of stories that emerge directly from people's experiences. Stories which enlighten; stories which challenge and move us; and stories that change the way we see mental illness and perhaps the way we see all of our lives. If we listen carefully to the stories and the poems that are gathered in this book we will hear new voices.

As we listen to and, more importantly, as we hear these voices, those whom we have chosen to call 'mentally ill' will be enabled to tell their stories well and, in telling their stories well, reclaim a vital voice within our understanding. This book will make a difference.

Rev. Professor John Swinton
Professor in Practical Theology and Pastoral Care
King's College University of Aberdeen

Table Of Contents

Foreword
About The Author
Acknowledgements
Prologue

Dedication
I Am A 'Normal' Person
A Beacon Of Hope
Shine Your Light Of Love And Hope
A Carer's Story
Dignity And Compassion
One Day At A Time
The Allotment
A Long Goodbye
Pastoral Care For Our Teenage Daughter
Living With Bipolar
My Precious Lord
Depression And Its Effects
Sink Or Swim
The Lord Does Not Disappoint
Empowerment
Mental Illness And Belief
I So Much Want To Die
Scared
My Family Is The Family Of God
Jesus Crowned With Thorns
Where Is God In All Of This?
A Bipolar Experience
A Mental Illness Observed
Kaleidoscope
Only A Miracle Will Set Us Free
Message Of Hope
Send Forth Your Spirit
Our Lady Of Mental Peace

Dedication

I forget when I first met Nick. I seemed to have known him for years. He would disappear off the radar for months at a time and then reappear as if nothing had happened. I usually met him when at a Conference or Information Day initiated by Social Services or MIND or other such organisation. It was when there was a mental health element on the agenda that both Nick and I would be there. A common interest. Over time and recognising each other at these events, Nick and I ended up in conversations together. He learnt of my first book published and wanted a copy. He followed with encouragement and enthusiasm my progress in raising awareness of the need for more pastoral support for people with mental illnesses and their families.

I was explaining to Nick one day about visiting parishes in the diocese in order to speak at Masses and taking my books in case any one wanted to purchase one. He offered to drive me to an outlying parish one weekend. He was so delighted to be involved and explained to me that his 'mission' in life was to change attitudes, to get rid of the stigma associated with mental illness, and to initiate more support.

To this end, Nick was very involved with the voluntary organisation STAMP (South Tees Advocacy in Mental Health Project), that existed to provide free, independent and confidential advocacy to people with mental health issues / problems, supporting them and empowering them to put forward their own views. The members met regularly and Nick was chair person for a number of years. Later it became STAMP Revisited ~ Independent Mental Health Advocacy Service and he continued being active in its service.

Over the years I learned that Nick was divorced with two adult sons and was a granddad. He developed bipolar affective disorder around the age of forty-five and had to give up work. Nick always had a very positive attitude about his disorder. He told me that he was never afraid to show his face to the public. He said that his mental illness could happen to anyone and that there was nothing to be ashamed of and he felt, that with good insight into it, it could be self-managed.

When at a low ebb, Nick shut himself away from the world and stayed within his home sanctuary where he could pray. Some time after I discovered the devotion to Our Lady of Mental Peace, I told Nick and of course he wanted a prayer card. He had a deep faith that sustained him throughout his life but especially through his years of mental ill health.

Nick was commissioned to minister as a Reader at church services many years after he was diagnosed with his illness and was told that he was a good Reader. He turned his back on this ministry when he found that the passages and the messages that he felt were for him 'spooked him out', but he was aware that this was because of his illness. When feeling more confident again, he asked to meet up with me to discuss how he might return to being a Reader, as his five-year commissioning had ended. We spent a very pleasant evening in a quiet local public house where Nick's drinks consisted of two cups of tea courtesy of the bar lady. I pointed him in the right direction regarding taking up his ministry of Reading again.

He wrote a prayer that I think speaks of his positive attitude, one that he dictated to me down the telephone line one day. I was so impressed with it that when I was completing my second book *Pastoral Care Mental Health,* I included this prayer at the very end. I showed the published book to Nick and he was delighted. He told others of my book and sold some copies to friends and acquaintances.

Sadly, earlier this year Nick died. I received a telephone call from his son asking if I would read his prayer publicly at his Requiem Mass. It was a privilege and honour to do so. Before I read his prayer from the altar, I told his family, friends, colleagues and acquaintances that Nick would not be forgotten, that his 'mission' would continue and that when my third book was published, I would include his prayer.

Your Strength Lord, Is Within Us

When the pressures of life are just too much
We just can't cope and really lose touch
From our illness there is no immunity
But you know we need your community
The people out there are our sisters and brothers
And what has happened to us will happen to others
This is your strength within us, Lord. We know it
We have your gift of compassion to show it
We pray to you, that we use it to benefit others
Your Church, and our sisters and brothers
Positive attitude to mental health awareness
Why the stigma? Where's the fairness?
Lord, we believe we understand the position
Give us your strength to work on this mission

AMDG
(Ad Majorem Dei Gloriam: To the greater glory of God)

Nick McCreton

So in memory of my good friend, I dedicate this book in thanksgiving to Nick for his enduring work in the realm of mental health and for his encouragement, support and friendship that he gave to me over the years. May his 'mission' continue to flourish. RIP (*requiescat in pace - may he rest in peace*)

I Am A 'Normal' Person

'Mum, how can you really believe God exists if he's invisible? How do you know he is not just made up?' Many of us have had that conversation with our children at one time or another. Many of us have that conversation with ourselves too. I know I do. But, five years after a very serious mental illness, I believe God exists by the very fact that I am still here. The intervening period has been fraught with challenges: coping with the ups and downs of living with three teenagers (albeit more joy than pain); the devastation of being deserted by a husband who apparently 'no longer loved me since my breakdown'; and then a life changing injury where I broke my back after an accident and subsequently lost my job. But, despite all this, I *am* still here.

My illness has brought me some blessings as well as challenges. I now know who my friends truly are. Some of those I loved most could not accept my illness or the person I now am. They cast aspersions, asked unanswerable questions, and then they walked away. Believe me, that hurt deeply. BUT, I have been blessed to have made new friendships. It is one such friendship that saved my life. I believe that God brought me that life-saving friend and for that I will be forever grateful. That friendship enriches me to this day and gives me yet another reason to *want* to still be here, living my life to the fullest.

I am still here for my wonderful children, for my family and my friends. I am still here for myself, because, on a good day, I can see that I am actually a worthwhile person despite my inner voice that so often tells me otherwise. My life has some value.

For whatever reason, my God chose me to be one of the twenty-five percent of people who has suffered and continues to suffer from debilitating periods of mental distress. And He chose me too to be a survivor. Why I may never know, but perhaps it may be so that I can do my bit in the fight against stigma and discrimination. Perhaps it is just so I can understand a little of how it felt to carry the cross, and learn some of Christ's humility.

On a black day, or a day when the immensity of my anxiety prevents me from functioning, my God is truly invisible. I cannot feel Him, or sense His presence. Despite that, I may rage at Him, I may curse at Him, and I have certainly been known to blame Him, but all the time, He is still holding me, whether I know it or not.

I am a 'normal' person. I am a mother. I run my own business. I am a school governor and a Trustee of our local MIND Association. I go to church when I am well. I can function just as well as you can. In fact you may never see my struggle with my invisible illness. So if or when you do, I ask you not to judge or cast aspersions. When you have walked a mile in my shoes, then, and only then, can you call me 'mad'.

Ronni

A Beacon Of Hope

'But how do you come through a depressive illness with any faith left?' The young woman eyed me honestly. She was the third person at that weekend Conference to have confided the same private anguish. I admitted that at times faith had been almost impossible, but I still asked how I would have survived without it. Then, seeing she was able to use her own depression creatively, I dared to add that sometimes I am tempted to think, 'what a waste of years'. But it was not. I would not be without that experience. For many still on this hard road such a claim makes nonsense. But others will recognise it as the essence of Christian paradox, when God is known by his long absences, and where the battle between being and non-being is relentless and the outcome unpredictable.

Looking back on my adventurous journey through a long depressive illness, I remember probably around the age of nine, asking myself: 'Are we trained to smile or is it natural?' The answer came swiftly: 'We are trained to smile because it is polite to smile.' No hesitation there. But even more indicative of my state (ever since I remember), was a strong sense of envy whenever a funeral procession passed by; and once watching from the top of a double-decker bus, wishing I was in that coffin on my way to 'pushing up the daisies'. It never occurred to me that this should have been of some concern.

I seldom shared my thoughts with anyone else, child or adult. I would describe myself as an almost mute child, painfully shy. My one form of self-expression was playing the piano from the age of six. I was allowed piano lessons when it was discovered that I was playing everything by ear learnt by my elder sister. I entered a wonderfully creative relationship with an extremely talented piano teacher who had fled the Russian Revolution and on reaching France had become Cortot's teaching assistant at the Paris Conservatoire before settling in London. She adored not only music but children and drew music out of me like a ready-made gift. A few years later she lost a ten-day-old infant and not long after, disappeared from my life with a long illness. Had I been allowed to know the truth, it was not as long as I had feared and I only found out when a visitor to our house remarked:

'Oh yes, she died, didn't she!' My mother had meant well by protecting me, but with my already strong religious beliefs (where from I never knew), I would have been far happier to have known she was with God.

Although with a wonderfully kind second teacher, through family circumstances, my piano learning came to an end. By the age of thirteen, I had lost my father to a complete mental breakdown (with the total loss of his two great creative abilities), my home and the Bechstein piano. On reaching secretarial college, I had an immediate fast typing speed, but found no real use for my hands until I volunteered at a Home of Healing and was straight away put to work as a nursing auxiliary. But by then I was aged forty. So what of the intervening years?

With hindsight, it is obvious I was a depressed child. By the age of nineteen I was in a serious state of depression. At first, I blamed burdensome circumstances, one after the other. Recognition of my own illness was perhaps the most arduous phase of all. Once there, however, intuitively I sought the right help. And somehow a 'hand-picked' team evolved, ordered, it seemed, by a kind of divine economy. Throughout, there was no searching for the right priest, therapist, or doctor. The number varied, when, for example, psychoanalysis was replaced by combined pastoral and specialised medical care in one person under the Healing Ministry.

I was totally unaware, from the amazing care I was given, that it was very early days for co-operation between religion and medicine. My Central London church, for many years close to my various places of work, became my mainstay, financing my weekly sessions of psychotherapy for over three years, at the instigation of its vicar, who saw me faithfully on a weekly basis, except for essential times away during an extremely demanding ministry. But always without fail, it was he himself and not his secretary who rang me if for any reason (and very rarely) he found himself unable to keep an appointment.

There were long periods when I lived on my pastor's unquenchable faith; undoubtedly the source of his faith in me, mirroring the person I was in the process of becoming. (I use the term 'pastor' for both priest and priestly doctor). Because of the devastating loss of self-hood, the principal team member agreed to act as my life line. With the ever-present danger of the vacuum I had become, only by this transference could I justify my existence while negotiating the gap I came to know as 'the abyss', and later, with Thomas Merton, that God himself 'is our abyss'. As many will appreciate, there is no hoodwinking the depressed person, no 'jollying' along. To have someone willing to remain alongside, who was not afraid to let me see that he did not always know the answer, lessened the gap between myself and the God who humbled himself.

I had little idea then that those were early days, since any notion of a future was inconceivable. At times, feelings of unreality and isolation were so acute that as I watched people speak, their voices seemed to come from next door. I remember the vivid archetypal images: the rider-less black charger of President Kennedy's funeral cortege plunging me into the abyss for several weeks. And there were days mercifully wiped clear with final healing.

But there was another kind of day, extremely rare but stupendously beautiful, bringing moments of transfiguration to carry me over those primordial waters... Once, having reached rock-bottom and hardly able to speak, I hid out in a convent in southern Cornwall where I was taken on gentle taxi tours of that breathtaking coastline by a lady mourning the death of her twin, because
'I can't be with anyone else... other people talk too much, I need your serenity'. A priest there, on loan from a distant monastery, brought the beginnings of order out of chaos:
'Before the world was conceived he had a plan for you'. The 'penance' he prescribed (Ps.18:19) provided the key to my true situation:

He brought me forth into a place of liberty:
He brought me forth, even because he had a favour
unto me.

The place of liberty I am still exploring over forty years on. Two years later, while on retreat in Kent, a chance meeting with a fellow priest brought me news of his stroke and subsequent depression.
'Please pray for him.' Ah yes, before the world was conceived...

There is so much more, including a dramatic breakthrough, which snatched me back from the brink one Good Friday... and final healing, which was simply a by-product of an even more profound experience - on the weekend I went to tell God I was packing Him in... But that is another story... The breakthrough occurred one Lent during my thirties, when, still suffering from severe depression after many years, I finally decided I must end my life.

For the past two years I had been receiving treatment, and my psychotherapist, himself a Christian, was closely interested in my spiritual state since it was almost always indicative of my psychological condition. To him, among other problems, I bore the burden of a heavy guilt complex; spiritually, it manifested itself in a hopeless inability to accept the forgiveness of sins. Knowing that without this belief I could hardly call myself a Christian, my distress was considerable. In addition, I felt divided from the Christ Himself, for in fact I had never got beyond the Cross; I had never known the joy of following Him through to the Resurrection. Easter had always been a mere formality.

As Holy Week drew closer, I knew with certainty that for me, this year, there could be no Good Friday devotions. I presented myself with endless arguments, but they were of no avail; I put to myself the questions of loyalty to family and others - which must so often torment people in this situation. I recalled that the only person recorded as having committed suicide in the Gospels was the one who had betrayed his Lord. But in the end I decided that, if I could not live through the Three Hours, I would at least die with Him. I laid my plans carefully and my farewell letters were written ready.

Looking For An Answer

In one of them I wrote:
I only pray to God that I have enough tablets... Though in thinking about this possibility that I may or may not succeed, I find I am looking for an answer to the question as to what life really is. Whatever the outcome, whichever side I wake up on, I am prepared to

accept that that is the life I am to live, and I promise you that if it should be that I am returned to consciousness, I will live it with my whole heart and never again question the wisdom of God.

In a last desperate bid, I opened my Bible, and the words that confronted me were those of Paul to the Colossians (3:1-3):

Were you not raised to life with Christ?
I repeat, you died:
and now your life lies hidden with Christ in God

In my letter I went on:
The passage is the one thing that puzzles me. I feel that the clue lies here somewhere - perhaps in the feeling that I am already living in death... But I am not really clear about it. I can only see now 'as though through a glass darkly'...

It was a few days before the light dawned, but when it did I saw what I had suspected was true: I had in fact gone through a form of dying. He had already placed me in the situation where I had promised to live life with my whole heart. What I craved for was not death but life, and the Life that Christ Himself, and only He, held out to me. There was no longer any need for physical death, since this had already been accomplished and overcome by my Saviour and it was unthinkable that His Precious Blood, which had been shed for me, should be wasted. I saw now how the only way forward lay through my acceptance of the Cross, the forgiveness of sins and the Resurrection, to the fulfilment of those promises which exceed all we can possibly desire.

I had taken a one-way ticket to the Good Friday Devotions, for originally that was where my life was to have ended, and I wanted my new life to start with a marked beginning - with the buying of a homeward ticket. As I emerged from the church after those glorious three hours, I felt as Lazarus must have felt on emerging from the grave. Everything was new to me; it seemed that the soft wind touched my face for the very first time. This feeling of newness to all things stayed with me for very many weeks, and a voice within me kept saying:

Behold, I make all things new!

Old Attitudes Gone

To the psychoanalyst, my changed state had come about through dying to my old attitudes and through my acceptance of life, towards which he had been working over the months; and both psychologically and spiritually, I had begun to find my true self. And the words that greeted me on that glorious 'first' Easter morning were none other than these, the words of the set Reading:

Were you not raised to life with Christ?
I repeat, you died;
and now your life lies hidden with Christ in God

My subsequent work in mental health started at a wonderful place in Bromley, Kent: The Stepping Stones Club, now, according to the latest telephone directory, Stepping Stones House, run by the Bromley Community Mental Health Team. In earlier days, attached to Bromley Hospital and overseen by a psychiatric sister-in-charge, it had been founded in 1946 by occupational therapists who saw how much mental health and other patients benefited one another. A host of creative activities took place there. I taught them relaxation, but later was much more involved: wrote a monthly newsletter and became a member of the Executive

Committee. To my surprise one day a fellow member told me:
'I always know which table (in the canteen) you are on, Felicia, because that is the table where the laughter is!'

Some years after my final recovery, I applied for hospital chaplaincy work in mental health and was sent to Warlingham Park Hospital, Surrey (sadly no longer extant) where I was given <u>nine</u> geriatric wards to look after. I arrived in November, not long before Christmas. No-one there knew of my previous medical history. Imagine my astonishment when, on first being shown round and reaching the Secure Ward, I was greeted by the male Nurse-in-Charge, who immediately said: 'The time here on this Ward we absolutely dread is Holy Week, when we hold our breath, because self-destruction then is at its peak!!!' I was speechless. My first thought was, are all the patients Irish Catholics? Did this apply to non-Christians as well? I would love to hear some learned feedback on this comment, some theological input!

I was involved with the Royal Mencap Society and worked voluntarily with one of their clients whilst still in South East London. An interesting comment when visiting / reporting back to the 'boss' in Central London: 'You are a practitioner. I am simply an administrator!'

On moving to Tunbridge Wells, I became involved in the work of the Crossways Community (mental / spiritual; health); and although no longer teaching relaxation, am still involved in two prayer groups of this wonderfully supportive organisation. My latest find though, through Crossways, is a remarkable Healing Centre on the Isle of Wight (non-residential, but devoted to mental and spiritual health): Carisbrooke Priory. It is great to have been led to these great Centres of Healing and to see the wonderful encouragement and support offered to sufferers such as I myself once was, and underpinned by such devoted care: thanks be to God.

Felicia Houssein

Five Good Reasons Why

Written after a Chaplaincy Course, this poem sums up experience in relation to faith. The rhythmic folk-song style reflects the youthful age of the five patients on the Unit

Perhaps after this, after this, I'll be able to follow more closely
How the Son of Man came to be slain
To see a little more clearly why He had to die

Only when the place you're in caves in
Can Truth, like a ray, splinter the dark, a flint of new fire ignite a spirited hope
Only then, out of its chrysalis, Life, however uncertainly, life re-emerges
Without it, I know I would have felt steel enter the soul and sharp edges of stones
Whose shouts could have shattered an eardrum or severed a nerve
And under a blood-red sky, the mind half-blinded, the heart deadened by grief
(His grief and ours), and I dead to His dying 'Yes' to five good reasons why
Yes, five good reasons why -

Perhaps after all, after all this
I'll find myself able to follow a little more closely
The Man who came to be slain -
To see in His scars the darkness of our pain -
And the darkness of our pain lift as the Son in us rises again
As the Son in us rises again

Felicia Houssein

Shine Your Light Of Love And Hope

I am organist at our local Church as well as being a minister of the Eucharistic. I am also Vice-Chair of our Parish Council. Our son has suffered from a psychotic illness for the last five years. Last Christmas he had to be compulsorily admitted under a section of the Mental Health Act. I found the experience very difficult but when I tried to talk about the psychiatric ward after Mass over coffee I felt people around me did not know what to say. It is so much easier to talk about someone suffering from a physical illness, but when it comes to mental illness, people seemed embarrassed to talk about it - I felt that I just could not share my feelings. How can we make mental illness an okay subject to talk about?

We saw our son today in the Mental Health Unit. His eyes were glazed over and he did not know whether he should come out from his cubicle. Perhaps his voices told him that he could not be sure of us... Perhaps he was just too exhausted after his compulsory admission earlier in the week, just two days after Christmas.

The entire world just seemed too much for him, as he turned back to his cubicle, lay down and tried to get some more sleep.

Lord, I have been trying to understand the terrible experience of psychosis in our young son. When the world feels so full of promise and opportunity, it is hard to understand that your creative goodness should pose so hard a burden on such a young life. When family and friends become too much and the bedroom is the only refuge for twenty-four hours a day; when nothing else matters other than retreating from the world.

Lord, we are back home now, in the darkness of the winter evening. Perhaps you can help us to find some meaning in the emptiness we feel tonight.

In the peace of our living room we have lit a candle for our son; it is next to the crib, symbol of your goodness and creation. Exhausted and bewildered, here we are, Lord, before you.

Help us to realise the goodness and personhood of our son who has been created and shaped in your own image.

Help him to glimpse once again a world of meaning and love. And in the darkness and confusion of his cubicle, be present to him and shine your light of love and hope.

Amen

Stephen

Writer's name has been changed by request

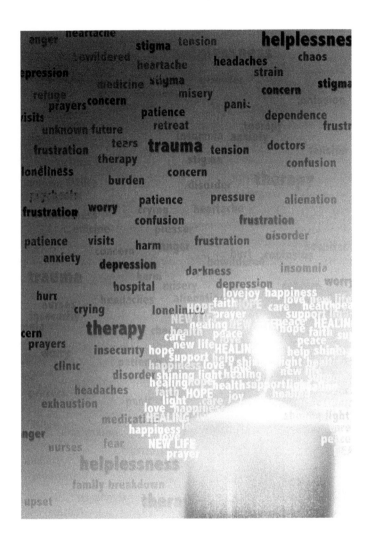

Shine Your Light Of Love And Hope

A Carer's Story

I have a number of brothers and sisters and, as a child, I was not aware that my mother had obsessive compulsive disorder tendencies. It was only later in life when looking back that we could see evidence of it. The disorder began to manifest itself more acutely in the years after my dad died, when my mother was sixty-two years old. I became the person to whom she off-loaded her obsessions, pleading with me for advice as no-one else must know! She made contact by regular telephone calls of an hour or more. Mam was clever and articulate with a great sense of humour but inside her four walls was tortured by her disorder. As I slowly began to understand the severity of her growing obsessions (scruples she called them), my attitude changed from frustration and annoyance to compassion and care.

Mam wrote a poem when seventy-five years old, after her second visit to a retreat house to which I had taken her for a few days, for a change of scenery and rest. Whilst there, she confided something of her illness to two nuns and a priest, her three friends. She knew her secret was safe with them.

Enough

Dear Friends, once again we'll be saying goodbye
A lump in the throat, perhaps a tear in the eye
And when you three reach the heavenly home
You'll wonder, 'Where's Muriel? Why hasn't she come?'
And you'll all wander out and stand at the gate
And I'll come plodding - and quite a bit late
And sheepishly smiling I'll say, 'Well, you know
I should have been here a long time ago
But I met with a scruple that stood in my way
As he often has done on many a day'

'You can't go up there,' he said with a grin
Your hands aren't clean and they won't let you in
You can't go to Heaven all dirty and rough
So just get them washed!' But I shouted, 'Enough!
You've cost me a fortune in tablets of soap
To tempt me again you just haven't a hope!'
And I gave him a kick. Where he's gone I don't know
But I think it's the place where I hope he would go!
So now that he's gone, let us all go inside
To that wonderful place where no scruples abide

This situation with my mother was on-going but manageable. However, it was when Elizabeth, aged thirteen and the youngest of our eight children, became very ill that life really got tough for me. After a number of visits to our doctor, I suspected something was seriously wrong and eventually, at an emergency appointment at the local mental hospital, we saw a consultant psychiatrist. The hospital was an old asylum but modernised, although its reputation had not necessarily moved at the same pace. (Recently it has been demolished and the new hospital has a different name). When I told Elizabeth where we were going, she was horrified. She said,
'You know what they say about that place, Mam. They call it the Looney Bin where the nutters and psychos go'. This kind of language is still used in our society. By turning a person into a label, we take away their dignity, their personhood and dehumanise them.

I was told that Elizabeth was very ill, in a severe clinical depression caused by a chemical imbalance triggered off at puberty, and she was to be a patient at the hospital. Everything had to go on hold, no school, no homework or music lessons. She was a clever girl. We had been told at her last Open Evening at school that she would probably do maths at university. She had passed five grades of cello and four of piano. She never again put in a full week at a time at school because of this illness. However, I was told that because of her age, it was thought that staying overnight at the hospital may do her more harm than good, that I could take her home each evening but not to let her out of my sight as they did not know her 'flip point', they said. In other words, she was suicidal and on a twenty-four hour watch. I took her home but I did not know what to expect. I was not a trained professional. I am a mother, a grandmother. That was early May.

The days ran into weeks and I looked after Elizabeth mostly at home with many visits to the hospital. It was very stressful for us, with Elizabeth's mood swings, broken nights and tears, and devastating on our family relationships with a lot of tension in our once happy home. In late June, Elizabeth spent her fourteenth birthday in bed in a severe depression. The psychiatrist had told Elizabeth to keep a diary of how she felt each day. This was one particular entry describing her feelings.

'I feel like an empty shell of myself, not my body, but my person, my personality. A transparent chrysalis with no choice of who I want to be or what I want to do. My life has been decided for me, to live every day as it comes with no meaning to life. I feel as if I am searching for the person I was and want to be, myself, but something keeps pulling it away. I sometimes get a firm grip on it, but it is slipping away. I can see a light at the end of the tunnel but it keeps dimming and sometimes even goes out. At times like that, I just want to lock myself away in a small dark room where no one can see the person I have become, the person who has fallen into a pit and finds it hard to come to terms with the fall. In this little room, I can heal and slowly grow back to the person I was and so long to be, to climb out of this pit. I do not want to die because there are so many things I love too much to leave, family, my music and my friends. Also if I did kill myself, I would cause too much pain to the people I love. I feel trapped by an unexplained tormenting presence.'

Elizabeth spent many days huddled in the corner of her bedroom, wrapped up in her duvet. Just weeks after her fourteenth birthday, she wrote a poem expressing her isolation and emptiness.

Changes

Changes are showing and you feel all alone
The silence growing; nowhere feels like home
Your life becomes night-time; no sign of morning
Hands out to reach you but still you keep falling
The hours of thinking; the hours of crying
So tired of living but scared of dying
You scream out longing but no one hears you
They just go on living when your life is dying
This strange sensation drawing you away
Making reality a stranger when you want it to stay

In August, three months after our first visit to the hospital, the psychiatrist wanted Elizabeth back because she was so ill and so I went to see a priest because up to this point we had not had a visit from one although they were praying for us but I needed a Christ-in-the-flesh. I asked the priest if he would come to our home and pray with us and our daughter. He was a kind and gentle man, humble and very honest. He said, 'Edna, I know my limitations and I am not very good with teenagers and I do not know your daughter very well. I was trained forty years ago and I know next to nothing about mental illness and I am frightened that if I come, I may do more harm than good.' I asked him if he could recommend anyone else and he said that he could not.

I went home alone. The stress was telling on me. I was slowly becoming a broken carer. I needed a compassionate Christ. I thought a lot about this. I think that we are a good Church at supporting families where there is sickness and suffering, and I suspect that had our daughter been experiencing a different sort of life-threatening illness, we would have had more support.

I met a Catholic neighbour and confided in her our daughter's illness and my need of pastoral support. She replied that when her daughter became mentally ill at University twenty years ago, there had been no support. I told myself that I did not want another person coming to me in twenty years time telling me that there was no pastoral support. I thought that the Church should do something about it but then told myself that as I am 'Church' and as I have had the experience, maybe I should do something. I vowed to try and change things.

I was doing my BA degree in Divinity at the time as a very mature student studying from home distance-learning. I decided that when I got my degree I would continue with a Masters degree because I knew I would be allowed to choose my own research topic and I wanted to look at this area of pastoral care within the Church. I wanted to see if there was a gap or was it just our family that I felt had fallen through the net.

As part of my research for my Masters Degree, I interviewed at length four Catholic clergy still active today in our diocese about support for families where there is sickness and suffering including where there are mental illnesses. I looked at Church documents that had been produced as a development from the Second Vatican Council (1962-1965) and found enough to support this area of pastoral care. I sent questionnaires out to carers' self-help support groups, one a 'secular' group and the other a pastoral support group that I had initiated with the help of a priest. Was there any difference?

The pastoral support meeting has been on-going ever since. It is a monthly meeting. We begin with a short Scripture reading because I needed to meet Christ in all of this. One day, a carer telephoned me. She said, 'Edna, I have been thinking of coming to your support group for some time now but I'm frightened that if I do, it will get out.' The stigma of mental illness! She did not want anyone to know what was going on in her family. I reassured her that what was said at the meeting was treated confidentially. She came and told her story. We share our joys and sorrows, and sometimes our tears and we conclude with a prayer.

I submitted all my research and the Examining Board gave me a distinction and said they hoped that I would get my research published in some form, which is what inspired me to write my book, *Carers in the Community: Why have you forsaken me?* re-published in 2009 under the title *Our Suicidal Teenagers: Where are you God?* It tells the story of the six years of our journey with our daughter through her teens, including her relapses, and the effect on our family relationships; how I went about setting up our carers' pastoral support group; of my ongoing support to my mother until she died; and includes my Masters research. The purpose of my book is, firstly, to give people hope because we are the lucky ones as we still have our daughter. Elizabeth eventually gained a place at University and in her late twenties was awarded her 2.1 degree at the University of Durham and is now a primary school teacher. She is married with children. Secondly, I hope the book will help in raising awareness of the effects of mental illnesses on individuals and families and hopefully instigate more pastoral support.

My second book, *Pastoral Care Mental Health* (2009) on pastoral care down the centuries, is the compilation of a further six years of part-time research, under the tutorship of an Anglican bishop who was a professor at the University of Durham. The book also includes results of responses, on attitudes regarding mental illness, to over five hundred questionnaires distributed to members of three Christian denominations across the North East of England; plus references to brief case stories in the final chapter.

After publication of my first book, I began to speak at Masses, at first in our diocese and then I ventured further afield to other dioceses. I have given talks at Conferences and to organisations. I have met many people on my journey and heard many stories. For example, I met a lady who has bipolar disorder and is unable to face her Christian community at Mass. I wondered how she received spiritual nourishment. I met a lady with serious depression who does go to church but is reluctant to speak about what her life is really like. I remembered the lady who initially came to our carers' meeting but found it was not for her as she was not a carer but a person with a mental illness. I wondered if she was still searching for pastoral support. I voiced my concerns to a priest and my desire to help. With his encouragement and support, I initiated another pastoral support group, this time for persons experiencing mental ill health in our communities.

In conclusion, I think people with mental illnesses in our society today are among some of the most marginalized people. They lose their self-esteem and their dignity. They do not feel very lovable and they have no status. Many people do not really want them in their back yards and as for applying for a job, do you put on the form where it asks about your mental health that you have been under a psychiatrist in your teens and / or still take medication and if so, will anyone employ you even if you are able to work? It is called discrimination.

I think if Christ was walking this earth today, He would be with these people and their families. He has our hands and our feet. So I hope that in raising awareness about the silent suffering that goes on behind four walls, there will be more understanding, acceptance, compassion and support, so that on the Day of Judgement, Christ can say,
'Come, you blessed of my Father. When you did this to one of these my brothers and sisters, you did it to me' (Mt.25:40).

Edna M Hunneysett

Dignity And Compassion

When I wrote to our bishop nine months into our daughter's illness, asking for advice on pastoral care where there is mental illness in a family, he pointed me in the direction of a local chaplain, Father Eddie Gubbins (now Canon). Father Eddie and I spent much time and energy sharing and discussing on how we might put this request of mine into action. The outcome was the initiation of a pastoral self-help support group for carers of people with mental illnesses, such as I was at that time. I was becoming a broken carer and needed spiritual nourishment to help heal the pain and emptiness that I was experiencing. Father Eddie firstly held a Healing Mass for carers and families. He facilitated our carers' monthly pastoral support group for many years and was supported by Sister Dymphna who worked in his parish. Sister Dymphna came faithfully almost every month for years and ministered to us through her gentleness, compassion, listening and sharing. Father Eddie also initiated a parish social event for those with mental ill health along with their families and friends. He only stopped coming to the group when he was moved to another parish. His pastoral ministry to us was greatly missed as was Sister's when we moved to another venue.

I asked Canon Eddie if he would put a few sentences together on this area of pastoral support. He wrote the following:
'As priest and shepherd in a town parish, I come in contact with people with a mental illness. Sometimes this is through parish visitation of homes or sometimes in the local hospital. I always try and see them as **a person with a mental illness** *not as a mentally ill person.* This is an important distinction. We do not say a broken leg person but a person with a broken leg, and so this should apply also to a person with a mental

illness. They are persons with beauty and dignity and who have rights. They need to be treated with the same care and attention as any other person.

Persons with a mental illness have taught me a lot down the years. They have a deep spirituality and love and dependence on God. The courage, faith and enduring hope they express is always inspirational. They are always reassured when, after patient listening, I pray with them or pray over them. This helps calm their fears and anxieties. In the Gospels, Jesus often meets with such people. He always treats them with dignity and compassion. He never fixes problems but always heals. This is part of my vision in ministering to them.'

Very Rev. Canon Edmond Gubbins
Diocese of Middlesbrough

One Day At A Time

There were around a dozen people at the very first coming together of our carers' pastoral support group and this was where I met Miriam. To put this more accurately, Miriam came to our very first meeting with another lady older than herself but neither of them said a word. We make a point of explaining that there is no obligation to speak at these meetings as I feel it takes great courage for some individuals to even bring themselves to come. They possibly make the effort after much deliberation when they are feeling vulnerable and desperate enough to try anything. I think that each person needs to be accepted and respected just as they are and only when they feel able and want to, I believe, will they have enough confidence to begin to explain why they have sought out the pastoral support group.

I did not know who these two ladies were and apart from welcoming everyone, I did not ask, but I do bring attention to the fact that people can join in and contribute as and when they feel they want to. I think it is very important to allow the individual to choose when to say something and not everyone wants to say who they are or why they have turned up until they feel they can trust the people around them. Trust is of the essence. We begin with a prayer and a Scripture Reading and following this, people are invited to share their thoughts if they wish. There is no judgement and no criticism or advice given unless someone specifically asks for ideas as to how to address a situation and of course individuals can then suggest or give information if they feel it might be helpful. This is all done in a very caring Christian atmosphere.

Each month, whether numbers were few or increased, Miriam and her companion turned up. I could see by Miriam's face that she was suffering and possibly ill herself. I suspected the other lady was her mother or a friend who had come along to support her. In fact we eventually found out that she was Miriam's mother-in-law. After a number of meetings and I guess it was when Miriam felt confident enough to come on her own, her mother-in-law stayed away.

Possibly around six months later and having attended each monthly meeting, Miriam found the strength and courage to finally speak. She began to tell us that her husband was ill and had been for years; that she struggled to bring up their two children alongside looking after him. Barely had she got this information out than the tears began to flow. My heart went out to her. Much later she finally told us, and even managed a smile as she spoke, that she had desperately wanted to talk when she came to the group but that she could not because she knew she would cry. I could identify with Miriam as I ended up crying at many of the earlier meetings but for me it was a healing process and I hoped for Miriam that in time the pain and isolation would subside as the support and prayer of friends around her strengthened her.

Bit by bit over the next months, Miriam released her story of her years of struggle and pain and her search for a pastoral group to help her through. She told us about her husband, Connor, and described him as a tall, handsome bloke who, when she first met him, was sociable, friendly and with a good job. There was no inkling that he was going to develop a serious mental illness. Miriam has a deep faith that means everything to her. In those early years when her husband's behaviour deteriorated and because she did not understand what was happening to him, she struggled on her own. She explained it thus.

'Connor and I married with nuptial Mass,' she said. 'We had a little girl and about three years later, a baby boy and both were both christened in the Catholic Church. Whilst they were still very young, Connor took ill but I did not understand what was going on. It was a terrible time and we did not get a diagnosis that it was manic depression - now bipolar disorder - until much later. I was on a new estate and there was no Catholic primary school near. It took me all my time to get to church. A priest came to our house to tell me that Connor had to stop telephoning the parish priest as he did not want to be disturbed. Connor had been doing this because of his mania. I went to ask the priest, who knew of our situation, if there was any help in getting our first child to the nearest Catholic primary school some distance away as neither of us drove a car then. I got no help. A health visitor got our little daughter into a local non-Catholic school early, as I was ill coping with Connor and our little girl and also our little boy under two years old, and the health visitor was worried about my health. No one came to visit although we kept going to church. The kids never went to Catholic schools because I did not have time to focus and my family did not understand about Connor. I struggled and Connor struggled in and out of hospital. So the kids never received the sacraments and it fills me with great sadness to this day and I pray that it will come right even though they are adults now.'

Miriam filled further gaps in her story to me. One of her neighbours worked at the mental hospital where Connor was admitted. It was a very old hospital, an old asylum, and recently has been demolished after a hundred years in existence and resurrected under a new name. Although it had been modernised over the years, everyone knew of this hospital's name, often referred to in earlier days as the 'Looney Bin' or the 'Nut' House, a stigma that scarred and damaged the in-patients and rubbed off on to their families. Miriam's neighbour who worked there told all the neighbours that Connor had been in the hospital and consequently these neighbours name-called Connor and the kids and shouted things at him in the street.

'We sold the house and moved in with his parents because of that,' Miriam explained. 'I searched and searched for a carers' support group but could not find any. I wanted to talk and relate to others who had experienced what I had been through and how important God is in my life and when in the depths of despair, I know God has his hand on my shoulder although it did not always feel like that. It was such a relief to me when I saw the notice in the church bulletin and came to the first meeting. My mother-in-law did not understand her son's behaviour although she did come to the meetings at first to try and support me. Connor is an only child and there was no extended family on his side to support me. My own family had too many problems of their own to be of much help,' she said.

Miriam came regularly for a number of years. She didn't just tell her story but listened and gave comforting words to others. She has a remarkable sense of humour that sees her through some of her darkest moments. She related a story of how her husband had a crush on a young lady, a well-known model who lived further down the country. In one of his manic attacks, Connor went off in the car and was not seen for hours. Miriam wondered what he was getting up to this time as he would draw money out and come home with a load of videos or other electrical equipment and then she would have to sort it all out.

'He just spends and spends when on a manic trip,' Miriam explained. 'So that is what I was expecting but this time I received a telephone call from a Doctor Miller. That's a new name, I thought. I have not heard of him before. He must be a new consultant at the hospital.

Connor must have ended up there. Not quite the situation,' she said. 'After a conversation with this doctor, I realised I was speaking to the father of the model that Connor so admired. Apparently Doctor Miller (and not a medical doctor) had found Connor skulking round his home and when he approached him and engaged in conversation with him, he realised that Connor was ill. He persuaded him to give my telephone number over and hence the phone call. The police escorted him back. You have to laugh,' she said, 'although it was not funny at the time.'

As is the nature of caring, some carers come for a while and some eventually stop coming for a variety of reason. Miriam made most of the meetings. These I hold every month without fail in case a new carer turns up unannounced and also so that the regular participants know that there will always be someone there to greet them. Sometimes one or maybe two people turn up and sometimes seven or eight. I like to think that carers know the meeting takes place without exception and the door is always open for them.

As Miriam was such a faithful attendee, it was noticeable when she failed to put in an appearance. Some months later, I met up with her in a neighbouring church hall for refreshments after a service. She was a visitor to that particular parish also. When I enquired after her health and that of her family and commented on her no longer coming to the support group, I took it that her situation had improved, hence her absence, and made reference to this. This was far from the truth. Miriam explained that the pressures of coping had gradually worn her down and she had succumbed to mental ill health herself.

'I went to see a psychiatrist,' she told me, 'as I knew I needed help. Now I am on medication. I am coming back though when I feel it up to it. To be in a Christian group is such a great help, just to be able to come and confide and also know it is confidential. It has got me through the worst days of my life. I knew you always made sure someone would be there even if just one. I knew I could pick up the phone and you would always be there even if I never did. I used to cry out loud to God, Why? Why? I cannot go on any more. He always sent the people, others not just you.' We shared some more. Miriam was certain she would be joining us again as she knew it was beneficial for her. It is quite a common occurrence in my experience for a carer of a person with a serious mental illness to eventually become ill themselves due to the stress and strain of coping with family life and traumatic situations.

True to her word, Miriam re-appeared on the scene at a later date. She was doing okay again, she told us, having her ups and downs but in better health and feeling able to keep going. She brings her wonderful sense of humour to the group and lifts our spirits. She is a great support and listens attentively to others and if asked for advice, because of her vast experience, is able to give it but always in her gentle, empathetic and unassuming way. Her children are now adults and she has a small grandchild.

We had grown used to Miriam, joining in month by month, welcoming and listening to newcomers that it was worrying to notice only a few months ago a decline in her health again. Miriam came to the meeting looking very tired. She had lost weight and was obviously struggling. She explained that recently her husband had been taken off his injections due to a culmination of side effects but had not been taking his medication orally. The distress Miriam was going through was horrendous as Connor was experiencing a manic episode and his spending of money over the internet was ballooning. He deteriorated to the point where the crisis team was called and he was admitted to hospital. He denied being ill and accused Miriam of 'putting him there' so that she did not have to look after him. Miriam explained how difficult it was to convince the staff that Connor was ill as he was so plausible when talking to the professional people.

'We have had a number of years of a relatively peaceful life and I cannot believe I am going through all this again,' she said. 'It was the old, old story of trying to make the medical profession understand just how bad things were, with Connor appearing to be in control. Luckily, I had kept all the notes of previous episodes of years ago and I fished out the file and was able to convince the staff of Connor's manic behaviour. I have been backwards and forwards to the hospital. Connor was placed in respite care as his physical health was not good and he needed therapy. I left for a few days' break but our son was aware of the situation and said he would keep an eye on things. However, Connor discharged himself and came home. The therapist continued to visit him at home but one day could not get an answer. The police were called and the paramedics and it was only when a neighbour reported that an ambulance had been seen outside our door that someone thought to check the hospitals. Connor was located in hospital. It is a running saga, isn't it,' she concluded, 'but for me it is one day at a time. God is good and we will get through.'

Miriam

Names have been changed by request

The Allotment

Lord, we wish to thank you for our beautiful allotment. We have been gifted by you with this green space where we gather with our friends, till the soil, plant little seeds, water the ground, relax in the sunshine and be one with all creation.

This is a place of healing and peace for us. We touch the earth, feel its soft moisture between our fingers, chat, reminisce about earlier years when we cared for our gardens and grew food for our loved ones.

The mysterious word 'dementia' is never mentioned at the allotment. We gather in our full humanity to work and enjoy the beauty of your creation. Birdsong fills the air and a gentle breeze brushes our cheek.

The allotment is a place of beauty and safety for many who share your cross, some struggling with fragile mental health; those at risk of isolation because of age or infirmity are welcome. We drink tea together and rest in your love. All is your gift and free of charge.

As we work we are reminded to be gentle with the soil as we remove the weeds that have threatened to choke the new seed; we wish to have a 'perfect patch', the neatest in our borough, to lead pure and spotless lives before you; in our desire to be perfect as you are perfect, we wish to remove anything that does not look or feel right in the soil of our lives.

As you know, Lord, we who live with dementia are highly sensitive and desire great beauty. You graciously remind us not to pull out the weeds,
'for in gathering the weeds you would uproot the wheat along with them. Let them both grow together until the harvest; and at harvest time I will tell the reapers,

'Collect the weeds first and bind them in bundles to be burned, but gather the wheat into my barn."

Lord, we thank you for your patience with us. We thank you that you accept us as we are, rather than as we feel we should be. We thank you that you offer us a lifetime of growth to become who you desire us to be. We thank you that you offer us this beautiful space where we are able to pray and reflect on your word. We thank you that our disability does not block us from hearing your voice but that through it we hear you in ever new ways. May we hear your word, share your word and live by your word in ever new ways. We bless you, Lord and creator of all, Amen.

Sister Siobhán

This reflection is taken from my book: Siobhan O'Keeffe (2011) *Petals of Prayer.* Kevin Mayhew Ltd, Stowmarket

A Long Goodbye

I first met Marjorie when she turned up at one of our carers' monthly pastoral support group meetings. I had changed the venue and placed announcements to this effect in various church weekly news bulletins. A different meeting place usually draws some new faces if conveniently near for them, as this one was to Marjorie because of it being in the parish room of the church she attended. I pay particular attention to newcomers by personally welcoming them and I try to help them feel at ease as well making clear that there is no obligation on their part to say anything, only when they feel they want to. The emphasis is on listening and acceptance in this confidential non-judgemental atmosphere. Marjorie, a smart and trim lady, of average height and pleasant face, in her sixties I would guess, said little, if anything, but it was rather crowded with some new faces and with one or two people anxious to pour out their difficulties. It can be a delicate situation as people are vulnerable and a little apprehensive at first. Some become tearful at finally being able to voice their concerns to a sympathetic small group. Beginning with a prayer and short Scripture reading helps, I feel, to place us in a listening and compassionate frame of mind. One carer also brought her elderly mother with her as she was unable to find a sitter for her. So it was quite a hectic meeting and I always wonder if the new carers will re-appear. After this particular gathering, one or more of the new carers came for a further few meetings including Marjorie. She has been attending now for a number of years.

Over the months Marjorie became more at ease with the other carers as she listened to them and she also told us about herself. She related how she came to realise that she needed some support, that she needed to talk to someone in confidence and that originally her intention had been to make enquiries at the local MIND Centre but on seeing the notice in the church bulletin, felt it was maybe an answer to prayer. She decided that she would come along to see if attending the pastoral meeting would be of help to her.

'My husband Harry and I have had thirty-seven wonderful years together years,' she said, 'but with no children are totally on our own and very much live for each other as neither of us has brothers or sisters. We have worked hard, are financially secure and we have many friends with whom we socialise and holiday together. It was when I began to notice Harry having lapses of memory that my attention became more focused on his health. At first, I put it down to age as he is a number of years older than me, but the pattern of forgetting was increasing and it was not just minor things. To give you an example, I will explain what happened two weeks ago, bearing in mind that he is a gentle, considerate man, and never one for breaking an appointment without notice, always courteous and polite, in fact what you would call a real gentleman. It was a bright and sunny afternoon when he left as usual to join his friends at the golf club. He really enjoys his games of golf, even more so after he retired. I waved him off whilst thinking how smart and pleasant he always looked and went back indoors to make myself a cup of tea. I am very proud of my husband,' Marjorie added, with a smile on her face. She continued with her tale.

'Half an hour later, the telephone rang and a voice asked if Harry was coming. I recognised the voice as belonging to John, who was a buddy of Harry's. Coming, I questioned and then added that if he meant for his game of golf, of course Harry was coming. I told John that Harry would not miss that for anything and that he left half an hour ago. Hasn't he arrived yet, I asked John. But John said that he hadn't and they were wondering if he was unwell. They decided to give me a ring to find out. I told him that Harry was certainly well, and eager to play. I thought this very strange as it was not like Harry to be late. John said okay and that they would wait awhile and then have a round of golf and hope he would appear. He asked me to let him know if anything was wrong with Harry.' Marjorie paused and the carers waited. You could see it was troubling her. She continued with her story. 'Harry had forgotten about his golf game at some point after leaving our house. In fact, he told me later that he could not understand how he could have forgotten. He never made the golf club and eventually arrived back home. We put it down to one of those things, a lapse of memory.

After this incident, I began to recall other instances of forgetfulness and it concerned me. I won't bore you with all the details but eventually Harry and I had a chat about his apparent lapses of memory and we decided to discuss the matter with our doctor in whom we have great trust. I think I knew what he was going to tell us. Harry was to have tests. He had a number of these, seeing different consultants over the next months and meanwhile he became apparently more absent-minded, wandering off at times without telling me where he was going. It was very disconcerting but I think I knew deep down where this might be leading us, about the nature of his condition. Eventually Harry was diagnosed with dementia. Vascular dementia. It still comes as a shock to hear those words even though I had my suspicions and was anticipating something of this sort. I then had lots of questions for the medical profession. I knew so little about dementia. Of course this is a while ago now and we have managed quite nicely but I am beginning to feel the strain and having no family, I really feel the need to share with someone who might understand.'

Over the next monthly pastoral carers meetings, Marjorie shared her journey with us, and it is a journey. As Marjorie says,

'Our lives have altered drastically. I am on a journey. There is no turning back. No plan. I take it day by day. As a person who is used to being in control career-wise and managing situations and people, I cannot control this and that is what has hit me the most, affected my self-confidence. The dementia has taken away his confidence. The carer role has overtaken the wife. He went into town this week, drove there himself as he still feels able enough to drive, but when he finished his shopping, he could not remember where he had left the car. I told him that he would have to give up driving and he agreed. It is becoming too much of a worry each time he goes out in the car and I get anxious that he will have an accident. We asked the advice of our doctor on this one and he gently told my husband that maybe it was time to dispose of his car. So it went. Harry takes this well. We share our sorrow over it. I feel for him so much as bit by bit he is unable to live the life he used to, is losing his independence and we no longer socialise as in the past. Another time, after this, he took the bus into town but then caught the wrong bus to come home and ended up further afield. So now we go together and regularly have a cup of coffee at a restaurant where we are quite well known. It is good to be able to keep some semblance of normality and share together as in previous times.'

At a later date, Marjorie told us of another incident that occurred.

'Do you know what happened last week?' she said. 'I can tell you because I know you will not think any worse of me because of it. It was when Harry and I went together into town as we do. I walked into a sweet shop to purchase a present for a friend and I spent some time browsing over the various assortments of boxes of chocolates and packages of goodies. Harry became restless and bored and so I chose a box and asked Harry to just wait by the door while I made the purchase at the counter. When I turned round, he was not there. My heart sank. In his frame of mind, he could easily get lost. I was in the large shopping Mall and I went to security and asked for a message to be put over the loud speaker. It carried throughout the shopping precinct and luckily someone, after hearing his description given out, recognised him wandering in the Centre. He was confused and a little distressed. We were reunited but I will not make that mistake again. It is a learning curve for me and I have to make decisions daily.'

In later meetings Marjorie continued to update us on their situation, allowing her to release some of her anxiety and pain. Her own health was deteriorating. She was becoming depressed and her sleeping patterns were changing. The stress was telling on her. With no family to support them, she and Harry decided that to give her a break, he would go into respite care for a week. The doctor thought this would be good for both of them. Marjorie was able, with research, to find a Care Home not too far away that she felt would be okay for Harry. They both inspected it. Members of staff were extremely pleasant and understanding and Harry was accepting that this was a necessary move for both of them.

'I visit Harry daily as it is quite close by and we enjoy a chat,' she told us, 'but I made another mistake,' she confided. 'On one of my visits, Harry asked me how I got into the Care Home as the staff had told him that the door was locked. I explained about the code for the door. He asked for the code number because he said he would like to take a walk in the garden and thinking nothing of this, I gave it to him. Two days later, I received a telephone call from the manager of the restaurant in town, the one that Harry and I frequented regularly. The staff were aware that Harry was not well. The manger said that he did not want to alarm me, but that Harry was sitting by himself in the restaurant. He said that Harry was quite all right but thought I might want to know and that possibly Harry may need help to get home. I was so grateful to the manager and told him I would be there shortly and asked him if he would kindly keep an eye on Harry until I arrived. I collected Harry and took him back to the Care Home and of course I admitted to giving Harry the code for the door. The code needed to be changed due to my lack of thought. I had not realised this would be the outcome of my telling Harry. He had left without telling anyone and made his way to a place of familiarity, the restaurant.'

Marjorie shared other insights with us that are a consequence of their changing circumstances.
'My faith in friendships has been shattered,' she said one evening. 'I thought I had some sincere and supporting friends of long-standing but they have shied away with no contact, as we are no longer a couple who can mix in this so-called social set. A result of my isolation and what has compensated me and helped me terrifically is this pastoral care group. It has been a saviour because through this church group I have met lovely caring Christian people who have enriched my life through befriending, comfort, wonderful support, giving me inspiration and strength to go on. Some of you have become very special because you are in regular contact as I now am with some of you, even if only a telephone call to enquire how we all are. I thought I was good at assessing people and I find the type of people I have met in this group has taught me at sixty-eight years old to be a better judge of character with more emphasis on the spiritual and Christian values than relying on people with material values. All this has taught me to be

thankful for what we have had and I have learnt the strength and force of prayer to help me keep going and God hears me and sends someone, for example, a phone call. I am still learning though,' she added.

As time passed, Harry began having fortnightly respite care, but the strain of looking after him at home without support or relief was taking its toll on Marjorie.
'I have made another decision, girls,' she stated one evening. 'Harry is going to go full-time into the Care Home. It seems such a hard decision but the doctor agrees that it is probably the best for both of us. I have pondered over this for some time but I do not feel I can be responsible for Harry on my own any more and I can still visit him regularly and take him out.'

She kept us updated at each meeting and then related another episode which clearly spelt out the deterioration of Harry with regard to his health.
'You know even though Harry is in care, I still take him each week to one of our favourite restaurants in an outlying village. We have done this for years and he continues to enjoy the food and familiar surroundings even though there is not much conversation. Well, when we went this week, he was unsettled. He was staring at the gentlemen on the next table eating their lunch. He then pointed to one of them saying that it was James, our bank manager, and that we ought to go and have a word with him. I glanced over to the group of gentlemen but Harry was mistaken. We were friendly with our bank manager and knew him well. These people were strangers to us. I said to Harry that I did not think we should disturb them and added that I suspected that they were having a working lunch and that we ought to respect their privacy. I was going along with Harry's notion of who they were as I did not want to end up in conflict with him. But Harry was becoming

insistent. I gently steered him out of the restaurant and into the car. It is so hard to see these changes.'

Later in the year, Marjorie explained how Harry was failing and shrinking before her eyes. 'Also, have I told you that Harry has now been moved to another part of the Care Home for more personal attention as he needs extra care?' She explained that it was no longer possible to take him out. 'Another step,' she said. 'When I visit, I just sit with him but conversation is limited. There was some consolation yesterday when I went. I asked him if he knew who I was and he told me that I was his wife, Marjorie, and that he loved me.' Marjorie looked around the room as she spoke these words to us and she appeared very emotional. 'I will not forget that, girls. It is something I can hang on to in my blacker moments. It will stay with me.' The five of us remain silent, allowing the depth of what Marjorie has said to sink in. I think we are all aware that the time will come when Harry will not recognise his beloved wife. We give Marjorie quiet for a moment for her private thoughts.

It was a few months later that Marjorie confided this to us.
'Remember what I told you a while ago about Harry knowing me? Well, I asked him again today if he knew who I was and he just looked at me and smiled but there was no recognition. I sit beside him and hold his hand. He is very frail. I like to think he knows that the person whose hand he is clasping is a person who loves him and that somehow this will bring him comfort. I am in bereavement, part one, of the man I married, and await the second bereavement when he finally departs. It is a long goodbye and I am sitting with pain.'

I telephoned Marjorie this evening.

'Harry is very ill,' she said, 'and I think it is time God took him. Harry does not know me but he has been a wonderful husband and I still love him. It has been a dream match. What more could I wish for? We have had almost forty-one years of a wonderful life. It is just a matter of time, now,' she says, 'and it is painful to see him.'

I conclude with words Marjorie spoke at an earlier meeting when she said,
'I know that ultimately I want to reach out and help others as I have been helped.'

Marjorie

Names have been changed by request

Pastoral Care For Our Teenage Daughter

Our teenage daughter has been ill this year, suffering from an eating disorder which was life threatening. Where do I begin to explain the feeling of anguish and fear of caring for a child with an eating disorder? I instinctively turned to my Church, to our diocese, for help for our child, this being the most natural thing for me to do. I just assumed there would be pastoral care in the diocese for my daughter. Our Youth Mission Team has been so prominent that I felt sure there would be something. However, sadly, when I asked I was told there is nothing for her. How can this be? I always imagined the Youth Mission Team were proactive and provided pastoral spiritual support. Sadly there is nothing for young people who are ill.

Through the Church I was referred to a lady in the next diocese, just over the border from ours, who works tirelessly to raise awareness for the need within the Church of spiritual pastoral care for our loved ones with mental health problems. Edna set up a support group for carers, praying together and sharing concerns and sometimes good news. This became Edna's life's work when she too discovered nearly twenty years ago that there was no pastoral care for her daughter who was suffering mental illness. Supporting carers and highlighting these issues has been her life's mission ever since.

I discovered, through a discussion on radio, a support group organised by a parent whose child suffers from an eating disorder. I did not know anyone in the group prior to the meeting and it is not a faith based group. However, the ironic thing was that I discovered every one there was Catholic! I believe this is because we are not afraid to ask for help as we are encouraged by our faith to seek help.

Our child still has a Faith but she now feels detached from her religion. She does not have that sense of belonging. Our spirituality is at the centre of our lives. In order to recover and gain a feeling of well-being, we all need spiritual support. Please God these issues will be addressed. We desperately need pastoral carers within our deanery.

From my own perspective, the experience has been an eye opener. Often it is only when we seek help that we realise there isn't any. Our world has changed and the pressures on our children have changed. Our Church has not had the expertise to cope with a lot of these issues. This is not a criticism of our hard-working and devoted priests.

Your mission, Edna, to have these issues highlighted, has been innovative and ground breaking. For me, I too have to take responsibility to change the support provision for our young people. So with that in mind I have joined our Co-workers within the Youth Ministry Team affiliated with our diocese. Together we are attempting to involve our young people and bring the youth to the centre of our Church. 'Thy Will Be Done.'

A Concerned Mother

Living With Bipolar

I have suffered a number of bouts of depression over the years, gradually getting worse, and have been diagnosed with having bipolar depression. It would be very easy in terms of talking about my depression to just look at the past few years and the more acute episodes, but, in coming to terms with being bipolar, and more of that later, I want to say something of my story. For it is only now that I can see that bipolar is something I have lived with for over twenty years and yet I did not know.

But firstly, I must tell you of Brian because Brian is fairly responsible for two important choices I made in my life, those of ordination and marriage. It was before Christmas nearly twenty years ago when I went to see him to ask what he knew about a lady I shall name Jacqui. It was after Christmas that after ten days Jacqui and I got engaged and we called to tell Brian who said something like 'Flipping 'eck'!! It was then a short while after, that I went to talk to Brian about being ordained. He said to go and see the vicar! At the time I was still nursing but I did go and work for a parish as Pastoral Assistant. On leaving, Brian presented me with a present, a book about clergy stress. How prophetic was that to be.

It would be easy when someone talks about depression, that by the end of it, we all feel like walking out and throwing ourselves off the bridge. I hope that is not the case. I am not an expert. However, I have struggled with depression for over twenty years, mostly without knowing, and in this account I want to share with you something of my and Jacqui's story, some of which some of you will echo with, recognise in yourselves or others, or maybe not at all.

I was brought up in Lancashire where the M6 is cobbled! School was a struggle as being deaf in my early years I missed out on my first year of schooling. I was thought to be just a naughty child at school until they diagnosed the deafness. My problem was that I could not hear what was going on. After that, I always seemed to be in catch-up mode. It was as if I was running a race and the finishing tape kept moving. I was, however, good at sport and music which compensated for me being near bottom of the class in other things.

After school I trained as a nurse, really enjoyed my work and, on qualifying, I first worked in a long-term care of the elderly unit before moving to an acute medical and stroke unit. It was to be here that I first experienced serious stress and depression. We were constantly under-staffed with very low morale. I had been asked to move onto another ward to help bring about change, after the work I had done on my first ward. No problem! It probably took about six months for my health to be affected. At first, it was just little things. Then it got to not wanting to go into work. Hoping you would be ill. Should I take this corner on my motor bike a bit too fast!

Then one day we had a death following an arrest. It was all unexpected and we did all we could. The patient only had his wife; no other family. I was told later by a member of senior staff that I had spent too much time with a bereaved relative. The following day, all I know was I was at home, and could not face work. My head was racing with thoughts. It was pounding. So I took some painkillers and just kept on taking them. I wrote a note to say I was sorry to my family and had failed people but this thankfully was never found. I was taken to the local A & E (Accident and Emergency) but not to the hospital I worked at. By this stage the tablets were taking effect and I felt hazy, like one of those dreams where all is in slow motion. My mum was shouting, 'My son has taken an overdose,' in what felt like the distance. I remember thinking that I know what is going to happen. I was aware of the judgemental looks, the sarcastic comments, as this thick plastic tube, like a garden hose, was forced down into my stomach. I had done this procedure myself a number of times as a nurse. I had seen it done on numerous occasions and been given to think: time wasters. Now here I was, a time waster. I spent a night in hospital and then saw the duty psychiatrist - said the appropriate things and they let me out. Nothing can prepare you for that journey home with a loved one, the silence of not knowing what to say, the feeling of shame, or talking about nothing as if nothing had gone on.

It was covered up in the hospital where I worked. Only the junior sister knew. She and her husband have been and still are very good friends. In fact I have these past few years discovered that her husband himself also suffers with depression. The management did not know what to do with me. Certainly no counselling was offered. That did not happen then. I had this feeling that I was an embarrassment - gone from being an excellent nurse to bad overnight, except it was not overnight. It was the build-up of little comments, doubting your own ability, setting very high expectations, feeling that others were putting high expectations on you.

Years later with the use of technology, I came across an advertisement on U-tube for Brigstone tyres: (http://www.youtube.com/watch?v=IpulJykYCOl&feature =related). It got me thinking about this event in a new way. These tyres are designed to save lives. As I watched the clip, and if you can, do so, I wondered what else had happened to that poor dog that this was the final straw, had to run away, get away, and then getting to the point that you just need to end it. But as the advert says: *saving lives*. That is what we each need. On this occasion I was able to summon up the inner strength to see that the way forward was to get out of the situation. To also look to my friends and most importantly discover who they were. I felt a shame that I could not share this with folk at church. Moving to a new situation; that was my life saver.

I then moved hospitals. This was a brand new start and no history; a completely blank page. I started work in a very busy operating department, throwing myself into the new challenge of learning new skills.

After some time and wanting to start another move and progress my career, I moved to another hospital to complete a post-registered course in theatre nursing. I should also point out that, during this time, I had a slight fall out with my local church and had not worshipped in church for two years.

So this was again a new page, a blank page. My career was going well. I found a new church to attend. I knew I had to go back because after coffee in the evening we went to the pub and I could get a good Northern pint. Things could not have been better and as I said, I met my future wife at the church, got engaged after ten days and then asked her how she felt about being the wife of a vicar!

However, the old pattern was emerging that whatever I did, it was a battle, a fight. My training was not straightforward, having to firstly complete a part-time course. During this, my first year report said I should not carry on as I was simplistic, unimaginative and vague! As I sat and read and re-read this report, all I could see was the word 'failure'. I was a failure. At the time I was working for a church in Derbyshire as well as doing some work with the prison chaplaincy. That day, by the time Jacqui arrived, I was absolutely plastered. I did not understand what was happening to me, or why I reacted like this. I should have led a Study Group that evening. Jacqui had to inform them I had a stomach upset. I was out for the count, drunk.

However, after chatting with a bishop, I came back with real fire in my belly, and took them on, playing the game, and was to come out of the course very well the following year, ready to start my training in Wiltshire for ordination.

It was a great place to live. I even had a visit from Brian and remember drinking coffee in the Centre. By the Christmas I was flying; entered into College life; delayed my essays to write the College pantomime! WOW! Things were great. I wrote a musical setting for the communion service which we used in College. I was flying.

But on the horizon was a fall coming. The College was to close. I was starting to feel doomed, that everything I touched, closed: my nursing school, my post-registered course, and two hospitals I had worked in.

We got to Easter. I was very involved in a team creating the liturgy for both the College and the Cathedral. I was flying high again. By summer we knew we had to move. So with a toddler and another child on the way, we arrived in Lincolnshire. However, the university would not accept my part one from the previous university I had attended; so another fight. It should have been me who was stressed with all of this but no, not me! I had boundless energy sorting it all out.

I became a curate at a church in Lincolnshire. This was not an easy curacy. Suddenly I was having lots of strange illnesses: chest pains that could not be explained; and back problems, making me have time off work. I remember thinking at times what a relief when the GP (General Practitioner) would sign me off. These were all signs of stress, without my knowing it.

We moved to Cheshire. I worked here with a great priest and it was just what I needed, but it was also the place I was first to be prescribed antidepressants. The shame! I could not get off them soon enough. What if people found out? I will never be made a vicar.

Well, I was made a vicar of two country parishes. It was only after I arrived that I discovered my predecessor could not face a PCC (parochial church council) meeting without dosing himself up with medication and he was an ex GP! A lot was made of me being the youngest vicar they had had in years.

In one community, the one we lived in, it was civil war, with school, church and community all fighting each other. I was looked upon as the one to solve things, and being my first post, felt under pressure to prove myself. I got stuck into many issues including a campaign to reduce speed outside school and helping the head teacher who was being bullied by governors and parents. Within two years we had a complete change of governors, as well as the head teacher. School went to having a waiting list for the first time.

But the bullying began as I began opening various cans of worms, fighting battles on all fronts. I could see myself starting to sink beneath the surface. Letters I received complaining about anything, from the state of the churchyard to the sound of the clock chimes and the PTA (Parent Teacher Association) car treasure hunt!

But then they started to get personal with abusive phone calls, and as rude as people were to me, I could not tell them to clear off. Imagine what the bishop would say! I was not sleeping, and when I did, my mind was racing. It came to a head as I was dashing one Sunday afternoon between the two churches. As I pulled into the village pub car park, I thought wow! They have been busy. It looks like a baptism party. Oh bother! It is! I had forgotten about it. The church was not ready. We got through as they were late and so we delayed things.

The following morning I was alone, in my study, sitting on the floor, in tears, screaming that I could not cope. I had been giving subtle hints about how the place was, the problems I was facing, without quite saying I could not cope because that is weakness. I found myself ringing the GP and he had a cancellation, so he could see me in one hour. When I saw him, I was saying that I could not sleep, that I was tired, that I could not cope, and admitting that I had been misusing prescription drugs. For quite some time the only way I had got through some days was with strong painkillers, diazepam and maybe some alcohol. Perhaps people thought the vicar was on a spiritual high. Well, he was actually spaced out. I allowed the GP to write depression and stress on the sick note.

The hardest call was to my area dean to tell him. Yet his response was very supportive and he came round to see me later that day. I struggled for a number of months, for there is no quick fix. I remember one day having thought I had had enough of all this. Life was not enjoyable. I got no pleasure. I could not concentrate on television or read a book. Even getting up was difficult. I took too many diazepam tablets. I then panicked. A good friend and neighbour took me to

A & E.   Then I would get well meaning Christian folk saying,
'But how could you be depressed? You are so full of life and enthusiasm; your faith'. That just does not help.

The pressure was on to get me back into work as soon as possible. As I was starting to get better, I decided one Sunday to clean my car. Some folks coming out of church saw me and wrote to the area dean to complain. He came to see me to tell me not to clean the car perhaps when people were around.

I was seeing a psychiatrist. Again this was hard to accept but she was great.

I was walking my dog in the field locally but she ran off and would not come back. Hell, even the dog does not listen to me. This was a turning point. I booked the dog in with a local dog trainer. Then one evening I went into church and cleared all the rubbish from the vestry, cleared the desk and made my mark. Jacqui was so worried about what I was doing in church that she rang a friend to go and see what I was up to.   When I finished, I stood at the church door, which was open, and rang the bell, shouting that I am the vicar.

I was ready for work again, or so I thought. The diocese said they would move us as soon as possible, but it was not convenient for the children at school. I had a point to prove. I was going to take this lot on and win. I had by now working with me a retired priest who was very wise. He came to the PCC and wardens meetings and was making notes. They thought he was 'helping me' but he was preparing a report for the diocese.

I did have another short spell off before we moved.

When we arrived in the new parish, I managed to get my new GP to take me off the antidepressants. Life was great and oh so different. But after about three months, I realised things were not too good with me; I was not sleeping, and was having panic attacks and anxiety attacks. I will be all right after a holiday, I told myself. That is what I need, a good rest.

It was during the harvest festival service in October that I broke. How I got through the service I do not know. The following day I went to the GP who straight away signed me off work and made a referral to the community psychiatric team. I re-started antidepressants but they were the wrong ones. On the Friday I went back to the GP with Jacqui who was able to tell him what antidepressants I had been on and they were changed. We had not heard from the psychiatric team. We went to see them in the afternoon.

On the Monday Jacqui was at work and this was the first time I had ever cut myself. I phoned Jacqui to say I had had enough and had also taken pills and alcohol. This meant a trip to A & E, but it is not like on television. I was becoming more agitated but I could hear, outside, a nurse saying how busy they were and that they had some psychiatric patients hanging around. That got me wild. Then the nurse came in to say that the cubicle was needed for some really sick patients. I nearly punched him. It was now that things were coming into the open more that I saw the love I was held in with family and friends. My mother-in-law came to take the children to her house for half-term, a real surprise and treat. If my wife was at work and I was not in the Day Unit, Mum or Dad would arrive and we would take our dogs for a walk.

There seems to be the two extremes for mental health patients in A & E. Either, acceptance, or we are in the way, wasting time. My illness was real. My pain was real. The only way I had to express this was by cutting and hurting myself. My brothers would take me into A & E, if needed, and as only brothers can do, would rib me mercilessly! For the three of us are known for our sense of humour and fun.

One afternoon while I was still working as a vicar, I decided on a plan. So I boiled the kettle and then poured it over my arm. Calmly I went to A & E. I had every intention of saying I had done this and wanted help. However, at reception, I found myself saying that I had spilt boiling water over myself while making a cup of tea.

'Don't worry, Father. We will sort you out.' It is amazing what a dog collar does. Yet within a number of weeks I was the time waster again. Taken in by my wife and brothers trying to access the emergency psychiatric team; no dog collar, just jeans, tee shirt and slashed arms. The attitude from some was so different. It made no sense to me at the time and even now I find it hard.

Locally we have this unit that I went to with Jacqui a couple of times for assessment. The children went to her mum's for half term. I was not even thinking about them and Jacqui at the time. On the Friday we went back to the unit which had three respite beds but I was clear I was not going into any psychiatric unit. However, a bed was available. Well, Jacqui needed a rest from me and so I agreed to go in as it was for her not me, I justified to myself.

The unit was okay and I had a nice bedroom. I was the only patient. This was the first time I had been asked about my faith. Was this a crisis of faith? In my bedroom that night I managed to self-harm again, opening up old cuts. The next day the nurse looking after me made me understand that if this continued, I would have to go off the unit. He was right. I came to really gel with him and it was after a few weeks attending the unit that bipolar was being mentioned. I attended the unit a few days a week, doing relaxation and group work. I have to admit that my preconceived ideas about psychiatric patients went out of the window. We were a really mixed bunch. As I improved, the medication was starting to kick in and again we talked about a return to work, a phased return. I started in April, so keen to prove myself again and light duties do not really work. By September I was off again. This sort of brings me to where I am today.

Last year was real crunch time. There was a point when I could have walked out on both my marriage and family. I felt so angry about myself, about what I had done. For a while I had no quality of life, no enjoyment. Neither did my family. My wife did not have a husband or the children a father. Jacqui would say she went to work for a rest. She was caring at home and working and was worn out. Yet I knew that I loved her deeply and could not make sense of this without her gentle and calm approach.

One of the things with bipolar is that spending can get out of hand. Mine certainly had and we had over seven thousand pounds worth of debt in loans, credit cards and bank overdraft. It is then hard to break out of the low mood spiral to start to take control of your life again. Jacqui realised the spending was getting out of hand when I spent nearly five hundred pounds on the computer in a week. She went to the computer shop to see them and instructed them that if I came in again with the PC (personal computer), to stall me and contact her, which they did. Many a time they would sit me down and give me coffee and talk and listen. We can laugh about it now and even this last week when I went in, they asked if I had spoken to the chancellor! I took the hard decision to cut up all my cards. I have to rely on Jacqui for money. That is really hard. I hope there will come a point in the future when I can control my finances again.

But I am not prepared to let it destroy my family again. When I was really ill and had self-harmed at home, our youngest child blamed himself by saying that if he had been at home, Daddy would not have done that, which, in part, was true. We felt we needed some support as a family. Then before you know, we are having Social Services coming to visit. This added stress to me and Jacqui, especially when they mentioned child protection. After a couple of hours interviewing all of us, they were happy the children were in no danger. They closed the file and case. I cannot tell you what that felt like.

My bishop decided to put me on gardening leave, which was a joke in itself as the vicarage was ninety percent flagstones. The congregation was told not to have any contact with me or me with them. The reason was that he was thinking about early retirement for me due to ill health. That was a blow and a set back, for me and for them.

By now, though, I was feeling stronger in myself. However, I would get very real anxiety attacks when out in public, especially if I saw someone I knew. I did not look ill. If I had my leg in a plaster it would be easier to have the time off. But if I was walking the dog and saw someone, I would be worried that they would be thinking that there is not much wrong with him, walking the dog.

The biggest blow was yet to come, when the archdeacon came to ask us to consider early retirement due to ill health. So that is it. I was to be on the scrap heap of the Church and only forty-five years old. What about somewhere to live; and income? I had so many questions. If I did not have stress before, I did now. I was told that free from the stress of parish life, I could have a new and creative ministry. However, the reality is a very restricted permission to officiate. I am working as a part-time chaplain at a local hospital for five hours a week. Strange to say that at my health screening with the NHS (National Health Service), my mental illness was not a problem.

So now I am very open about my illness. That way they can understand how I react, my changing moods. If people ask how I am, I answer honestly, which can come as a shock. I still struggle to understand what my ministry is. I have been invited to be on the Disability Action group in the diocese.

There is the possibility I will be speaking at the National Conference of Inclusive Church. I want to say that an inclusive church is a lovely place. The reality has to be a place that enables debate and discussion in a non-threatening way, which may be uncomfortable. But which of those places do you really want to be in? A place of false smiles and shallow conversation or the place where you are accepted for the person you are and all that you bring? Which then by its nature is inclusive and loving?

My story has not ended but I am learning to become me in control of my condition and recognise what is happening. That is why I am open with folk, so that they understand, just as a person with diabetes would make people aware of their condition.

One of my favourite passages of Scripture is the post-Resurrection account of the two disciples going to Emmaus. Jesus accompanied them but they did not recognise him. I have been accompanied on my journey by some very special people in family, friends and healthcare professionals.

I hope that in sharing my story, it will encourage and help others either to be accompanied or to be the one who walks beside, listening.

Helpful web sites
http://www.mind.org.uk/help/diagnoses
and_conditions/bipolar_disorder_manic_depression

http://www.mdf.org.uk/?o=56878

A struggling Anglican Priest

Names have been changed by request

My Precious Lord, I'm In Despair

My Precious Lord

Freedom (1985)

I sit looking out of the window, at people passing by
Oh why can't I be one of them? I say to myself, and sigh
What good does it do to stay inside, feeling frustrated,
alone and afraid?
I must turn the key and free myself from this prison I
have made

I know it won't be easy but at least I'm going to try
I don't intend to sit around and let life pass me by
One day when I am free again and I know that day will
come
I pray to God that I may help some other 'anxious' one

Tormented (1986)

I can't stand it any longer. I just don't know what to do
I cannot sit. I cannot lay. I walk around the house all
day
My mind's in such a muddle. My body's in need of rest
My husband doesn't understand though he tries his very
best

The kids are fighting and screaming; their dinners fell on
the floor
I know I've got to get away, but I daren't go out the door
If only my mind could be peaceful and my stomach not
tied in a knot
I'd be so happy and contented. Am I asking for such a
lot?

My Precious Lord (1990)

My precious Lord I'm in despair
As everything around me looks dark and bleak
Both my mind and my body are feeling so weak
Dear Lord up above, please give me the strength and
the will
Let me feel Your presence near me while I'm low and
feeling ill
Dear Lord I'm lost. Show me the right road to go
You are my Shepherd: guard me through the winds and
the snow
Dear Lord, take my hand and guide me today
Show me the light and show me the way
My Precious Lord, You are my Saviour and my Light
Give me strength, give me courage; help me through
this dark night

At the time of writing these poems I was in a very dark place. I still struggle with anxiety today but I find strength from my faith in God. He is my comforter, my healer, and my deliverer. Going to Mass and receiving the Eucharist as often as I can help me to cope with everyday life.

Patricia Frewin

Depression And Its Effects

I think the best way to describe depression is unfortunately to have had it yourself, which is not recommended, believe you me. I would say, and indeed anyone who has had this horrible disease knows, how very devastating it is to one's whole being. From my own point of view as a strong Catholic, it took the Blessed Lord away from me, and this was the most dreadful thing that could happen to me and indeed any Christian and it took seventeen weeks to have any counselling through my own doctor, and that is absolutely scandalous. The way a person feels when in this state, especially if it is severe, could cause a person to end their very life!

I am sure that the National Health Service, when it began, was all well intended, but these days things have all gone terribly wrong. It seems to me that because it is not supported financially well enough and very badly managed, it is falling apart and everyone knows it but nothing seems to be getting done about it. In my opinion, I think they should have Matrons back on the ward (my husband suggested they should all be like Hattie Jacques - he has, thank God, got his sense of humour back again) as, when I was in hospital recently, there were some nurses talking and laughing at the desk, and they could be clearly heard.

I also found some of the nurses did not have enough compassion and I developed one of my serious bouts of depression when in hospital that particular time. The hospital I attended is very much a university hospital, I am afraid. From a surgical point of view, they, I think, cannot be faulted, but from an emotional point of view, they are very sadly lacking. The most important thing when you are ill is to have lots of compassion and if I had anything to do with it, would not employ anyone as a nurse or doctor if they were lacking in this emotion. I am not the only person who feels this way; there are many people who find this to be the case. Anyway, I am getting off the subject a little here.

To continue about depression, I found that when morning came, for instance (and this is when I was taking medication), that I could not face getting up at all; I wanted to just sleep and sleep. When I finally did get up out of bed, I would struggle to wash myself and eat something my husband had put out for me. Also, he would make my sandwiches for lunch and I would just lie down on the sofa all day watching television or reading something light. When he came home from work, I would have a pan full of meat and vegetables (usually the same thing every night) for tea and it took me a great deal of effort just to do that! The life of a spouse is not to be envied when the mind is in such a low state I would say, but I have certainly been very blessed by God to have such a wonderful husband.

Now The Stranger: Your Wife

A man having to live with a wife with depression finds life very, very difficult, if not to say almost impossible. The woman he married is now very dependent on him, almost childlike in her behaviour. Her personality totally changes at that time. His home, that used to be his sanctuary, is now a place of misery. No longer is the life he now lives with his wife the same as before, but in fact almost the opposite. His wife is now totally inconsolable and he finds it impossible to help her out of the kind of hell she is going through. He can hear her crying and repeating worries over and over and there is nothing he can do about it. This is all very upsetting for him to see his wife in such a distressed state, and no matter how many times he tries to console her, he cannot make any difference to her behaviour. He may very easily slip into depression himself, and what will happen then? There has never been a more important time for the Church to support them than now.

When people are physically ill everyone gives them their support and rightly so. Not so with mental illness though, as people feel too embarrassed to tell anyone because of the terrible stigma attached to it. If only people could see this. Understanding is so very important at this time as families of the person who has depression need lots of support, more than ever before. Unfortunately there are, I think, a lot of people who think you should be able to pull yourself out of it. As if you have some choice in the matter. I only wish that was the case. It is like something has locked up your mind and you are no longer responsible for your feelings. All of them are sad, not one happy one left.

The mind is such a delicate thing, as when dwelling on something that makes you sad, it can go further and further down, into the very bowels of hell it seems. The answer, therefore, is to make sure you do not do this. However, when in depression, your mind is so cut off from Him, and for a Christian in particular, this is totally devastating. Keeping very close to God is indeed a very good insurance against it; in fact it is <u>the</u> one!

Having a balance in life is so important to us all. There are many ups and downs and so we have to make sure we make time to do something we enjoy every now and then.

Here Is God

Your life can be hell, if you sit and dwell
On the things that have got you quite down
We all know those things that are varied and bad
So easy to shake us and make us so sad
But staying indoors and covering up
Make them all so much bigger than they really are
And the pit is so deep with no way out sign
And the walls which are slippery and wet
Make it all so much harder to rise from the depths
Of the darkness so thick and so dense
And it sucks you right in; you go deeper and down
And it swirls you and drags you around
And you feel you are nothing, an invisible thing
A worthless, a nothing, a fool and a clown

But if you pray to God, there's a bright shaft of light
Though very much hidden from view
Then the darkness dispels and the sun shines right
through
And warms you and lifts you and joy comes right in
And your world opens up and it widens and deepens
And you feel love arise (at last) and it opens your eyes
To the love and the joy that stays and abides
Deep in your mind and yes, here now, is God!

The trouble is that it is not always possible to 'tune in' to
what God wants of us when the mind is so low, and we
need to realize this, and not worry while our mind is in
such a low state. God has so much more patience than
any of us will ever have. So therefore we must be
patient with ourselves, just like our heavenly Father is,
and just quietly wait, as He will put everything right in his
own time. God Bless.

Jean Leyden

Sink Or Swim

1st June 2004
To whom it may concern (A covering letter from Maggie's mother for a College application)

I am writing to inform you that Maggie did not take her GCSEs (General Certificate of Secondary Education) in Year 11, owing to illness caused by family difficulties during the previous two years. Prior to these difficulties, Maggie was an able student, usually in the higher groups in her year and forecast to get good grades in her final exams. A summary of the circumstances is as follows:

- *Following a breakdown in relationships between her father and mother (myself), Maggie and her brother had to remain in the family home whilst the house was redecorated and put on the market, a long drawn out process, taking over a year.*

- *The actual divorce proceedings took from March 2002 to February 2003, during which time her father moved out to live with his new girlfriend, moved back when they had a disagreement and moved out again. The whole proceedings lasted two years, included mediation for residency of both children, and were extremely stressful for all concerned.*

- *During the final few months of the house sale she lost two near acquaintances, one in her age group to suicide and one - a neighbour's daughter she had grown up with - to a road accident. As the house sale was being finalised, her paternal grandfather died.*

After moving house at the end of summer 2003, to live with her brother, mother and mother's new partner, Maggie was physically and emotionally exhausted. She began missing school for headaches, sickness and stomach aches; was reluctant to leave home and suffered from a total lack of energy. She was eventually diagnosed with depression and put on medication.

In December 2003 Maggie moved to live with her father, his new partner and her two children, a few miles away. Her father obtained a place for her in Year 10 in a new secondary school. Unfortunately, although she made a good start in January 2004, she was unable to maintain the effort required to attend school full-time and found her new home circumstances difficult. After a serious disagreement with her father in February 2004, she chose to return to live with her mother. The stress caused by this unsettled period resulted in a return of her depression. She was unable to continue attending the new secondary school on a regular basis and the pressure to do so was having a detrimental effect on her health. As she had been placed in year 10, she had not been entered for any of the GCSEs she would normally have taken at her age.

Eventually after very careful consideration of all possible options, it was agreed that Maggie would go and stay with her maternal grandparents for the last few months of the summer term. They would supervise her studying at home for the remainder of the school year and, being semi-retired, were in a position to give her much more support than was possible with both her parents working full-time hours.

This decision put Maggie on the road to recovery and although she is still on medication for depression, she is taking a more positive view of her circumstances and is

*now determined to continue her education with her own
age group.*

*I hope that this clarifies the situation
Yours Sincerely
Kate Hodgson*

Maggie's Story

My favourite lesson in life will always be, 'that which
does not kill us will only make us stronger'. Why? This
is because as cheesy as it is, that is pretty much how I
have learnt to deal with life. In my twenty-two years on
this earth I have not broken a bone in my body
(although I did come close to slicing off a toe at the age
of five). I live in a town house in the North of England
that I share with my friend, her five pet rats and my
puppy. I am currently studying for a BA (Hons) in
photography which I am hoping will help develop into a
career in photojournalism. I have not always been so
determined though. If you had asked me at a younger
age what I wanted to do later in life, the response would
have been my sweetest smile and, 'I haven't made up
my mind yet'. The truth is though, it was a forced smile
and I would have been wondering if anyone would
notice if I killed myself tomorrow. When I was fifteen
years old I was diagnosed with reactive depression but
we will go into that later...

To tell you a long sob story of being a neglected child
would simply be a lie. I was brought up by both my
parents with my younger brother Ray and more pets
than I could ever recall all the names for. We attended
a good school, had plenty of hobbies and friends and
were loved dearly by all the family. Admittedly I was
bullied in primary school but then most kids are at that

age. The transition into secondary school went smoothly and throughout my time at school I kept a high grade average. Most of my friends would bounce in and out of 'relationships' like any other teenagers but I was not really fussed about boys until my mid teens and even then I think I only had two boyfriends throughout my time at school. I cannot really pinpoint exactly when I got ill but I guess it was when things between my parents started to change. I had already seen what a split home does to teenagers because a friend from school had suffered her parents' divorce at the end of Year 8. It is always different to experience things on your own though.

My first realisation of changes to come was the same night David Sneddon won Fame Academy. It is strange which memories the brain will let you keep. I remember my dad putting some kind of rota on the kitchen notice board for family days out, like where we were going etcetera. Apparently we had gone from being a family to just four people living in the same house and he wanted it to change because he was scared we would fall apart. He was so upset. I know that night I sat on MSN (The Microsoft Network) to my friend (with the split home) and sobbed for ages. I am not too sure the rota worked though because the only day out I can remember was going to London with my dad and brother while Mum took a shift at work.

There was another day when Mum came home with a rose and put it in a vase in the dining room. This was very rarely used; it was more like a valuables storage room than a family dining area. The flower was from a man at her work and I know it seemed weird at the time but I guess I just shrugged it off and got on with my own thing. This was back in 2002. That was the summer I 'mastered the art' of crying so no-one could hear and I know most nights I would cry myself to sleep. It was also the summer my maternal grandparents came to visit and the news that my parents were separating was broken to me and my brother. I know Ray was really upset and cried a lot during the talk and I remember feeling guilty at the time for not showing much emotion but, to be honest, I had cried so much beforehand that it was as if I had lost the ability. After that, Mum moved into the spare room and things pretty much went back to normal.

September 2002 was when the first part of my parents' divorce came through, actually on my fifteenth birthday. Both my parents got me lots of little presents but the main one from each of them was an Eeyore mug from the Disney shop. They hadn't even discussed with each other what they were buying. But hey, it was only another birthday.

By Christmas things had totally changed. Dad had moved in with a new woman and her kids. Mum spent a lot of time with her fella from work. Christmas day was weird. We had present opening together as a family for the last time and Mum went to her boyfriend's house for lunch. This left just the three of us for our Christmas spread. It is only from looking back at photos that I remember this, and I always feel bad for doing so because even though there are smiles all round, my dad's eyes are red in all of them from holding back tears. I had not noticed at the time. The finalisation of the divorce came through on February 14th 2003 which was also the day our next door neighbours got married. It seemed funny to me how the two homes so close to each other could be experiencing two complete opposites in the marriage line.

Shortly after, my paternal grandparents jetted off to Italy for two weeks, which was pretty normal as they often travelled to 'exotic' places. Apparently though,

Granddad came down with food poisoning towards the end of the holiday. He was quite poorly by the time they got home. Time was not a healer though and eventually he was admitted to hospital for tests. During this time his kidneys packed in and he caught MRSA. No-one was massively worried at this point as he was acting okay and seemed to be reacting well to the medication and dialysis.

Things at home had got pretty crowded though. It was decided that the family home was to be sold and Mum and her boyfriend wanted to get a place together. Rooms were painted magnolia, possessions boxed as much as possible without disrupting school work and the house was put on the market. To this day I still refuse to have magnolia on the walls in my home. By the time we had broken up from school for the summer, Mum's new man had moved in until we found a more permanent house for us. It took ages to find a new place and get contracts signed but we got there in the end and were due to move just after we went back to school.

That summer I spent most days keeping busy with a friend from my tutor group. She had a massive crush on one of the guys two years above us who was a mutual friend of ours. It just so happened that Gary had recently got a job at the local bowling alley and my friend suddenly got very interested in playing pool on a regular basis. It was obviously in the hope that we would catch a day he was working. I did not mind as it meant I was out of the house. He was easy to get on with too and if we were there at the finish of his shift, I would end up walking home with him as he lived just down the road from me. It was never for long but it was so good to just escape the reality of the chaos going on at home.

Throughout the summer Granddad seemed to gradually get worse and eventually lost the battle. It was my dad who phoned to tell us. I answered the phone and he asked for my mum. As soon as I had passed over the phone I knew Granddad was gone. I texted my boyfriend at the time to tell him and to this day I still have the image of Jamie quite literally running down the road to be by my side. For the rest of the day we watched films and snuggled up on the sofa. Mum bought KFC (Kentucky Fried Chicken) for everyone to try and lift our spirits. Any tears shed that day though were probably more of relief that he was not in pain any more. I never went to visit him at the hospital because I did not want my last memories of him to be as a frail old man hooked up to machines. I think I also expected him to get better. We sent him a 'get well soon' card when he was admitted to the hospital which I later found in the bedroom I slept in at Gran's house. I remember reading it and thinking what an idiot I was for not going to see him and hoping he did not think any less of me for staying away. I had attended a few funerals when I was younger but I had never been to one for someone so close and I found it quite hard. The service was held in a very small, very cold, grey church. He was cremated. Therefore, there was no graveside service and the whole day seemed to fly by.

We returned to school in September and moved house just two weeks after going back. This is where I definitely started to show signs of depression. I did not return to school the Monday after moving due to pure exhaustion but I started to get a lot of headaches and sore throats and my chest began to tighten. I was off school for quite a while. I was tested for glandular fever but the results were negative. The doctor tried all sorts of gastric remedies thinking it was my digestion and not my chest, and I probably had some sort of antibiotic for my throat. I would manage to go to school for a couple of days a week but still felt really bad. It was so frustrating feeling so pathetic all the time, and when friends sent texts to me to ask how I was, I just ignored them because I could not be bothered with texting back. I stopped leaving the house unless I had to and most of the time Jamie would come to me.

I think somehow I have managed to block a lot of this from my memory. It is so hard to recall details but I definitely remember my first panic attack. Jamie and I had broken up over the phone the day before and I asked him to meet me to discuss things face to face. Apparently there was no going back and when I got home I absolutely sobbed my heart out. I must have really worked myself into a state though because the room was spinning and I could not catch my breath. Poor Mum sat with me the whole time to reassure me but I was having none of it. I felt absolutely terrible and that night I genuinely thought I was going to die.

About a week later my maternal grandmother came to visit with my auntie Grace and her two kids. When my auntie was a teenager she was diagnosed with clinical depression but she has come through her own battle with the illness. I think because of her background she was pretty quick to notice something was wrong. I remember being off school for a few of the days they were visiting and on one of them Grace had confronted me about how I was feeling. She asked if I had thought about self-harming and whether the world would continue without me. The truth was I had. It was so good to be able to talk to someone who understood how I felt. I could not talk to my friends; they just would not understand. Everyone at school just assumed I was bunking off because I had been dumped and so I was in no hurry to get back to people who obviously thought so little of me. At least that is how it felt. I went through half a toilet roll from wiping away tears and blowing my nose. We both laughed about this later. One memory that will always make me giggle is that whilst staying, my little cousin William was sitting in a cardboard box eating Cheerios (you know how small children love empty boxes). He was rocking back and forth and without warning the box toppled over. When we put it the right way up, William was sitting with the cereal bowl on his head and Cheerios in his hair. It was very much a 'You've Been Framed' moment. Also whilst visiting, his sister Aimee had drawn a picture of a kite for my mum and stuck it to a wall using Pritt Stick. Mum spent weeks picking tiny bits of paper off the wall once they had gone.

Grace had advised Mum to take me to the doctors. An appointment was made but I could not tell you the details of what was said. I know Mum took some time off work so that I was not left alone. I would go everywhere she went; I was like a lost lamb. Shopping trips were my favourite because it was always just me and her. On one trip though we bumped into Gary and his new girlfriend, who asked why he had not seen me around school for a while. I filled him in on everything briefly and the look of sympathy on his face was too much to bear. After that I was so ashamed and the stigma of being 'mentally ill' ate away at me. It was as if I walked around with a giant neon sign flashing over my head advertising that I had suicidal thoughts. I felt so vulnerable and aware of my surroundings; it was like every stranger who walked past knew I was sick and would stare like I was an alien. In reality no-one ever looked twice but the paranoia overtook reason.

I remember being forwarded to a child psychiatrist and having to fill out a really personal questionnaire. I was quite glad that it had its own envelope because there were things asked that I did not want my mum to know. I think even back then I was quite protective over her and did not want to upset her with worrying over me. I was also prescribed Seroxat and had to return to the doctors every Monday morning so he could check I was adjusting okay. I do not know if the tablets were ever meant as a long or short term cure but I know that when we went to pick up the prescription the chemist came out to talk to us. Apparently Seroxat had a bad reputation and was only intended for over eighteen year olds (I was only sixteen). Looking back now with the knowledge I have on that medication, I could say I probably owe that man my life. At the next doctor's meeting, Mum pushed for a drug change and I was switched to Prozac.

When you have a teenager who does not attend school under the age of sixteen, then eventually you will get social services on your back. I am not blaming anything on them but when they inform you of the ridiculous amounts of fines you could face, it is bound to push a depressed teen to suicide just to get the parents out of trouble. I can't ever remember attempting suicide but cannot say the thought never crossed my mind. I was pushed back into a school routine but after a meeting between my mum and my Head of Year it was decided that certain subjects were to be dropped to ease myself back into the classroom. All my teachers were informed of the circumstances and extra support was offered.

One lesson that sticks out in my mind was English one afternoon. We all went into class and the lads behind me both bugged me for the reason why I was absent a lot. I shrugged them off and blamed the glandular fever tests. When the teacher handed out work books, he tried to reassure me to check I could cope with the workload, and I know he was only doing his job but I felt like an absolute freak.

Shortly after, a new technique was tried so that I was in school but could stay out of the classroom. At our school, whenever someone was out of order or a teacher could not cope, said child was sent to the 'Isolation Room'. This room had been located next to my old form room; so I had managed to glance in once or twice. There were literally five or six desks that had single cubicle space. It was a tiny room with one frosted glass window and was painted white. Basically you had to be a complete brat and bully to be placed there. However, the rules on these rooms had been changed. When we returned to school that September, one of the sixth-form common rooms had been moved and the old one was turned into a 'Supported Learning' room. This was to encourage better behaviour I think but it was also where slower students were put for one-to-one learning. This room was their alternative to help keep me in school.

I know everyone was trying hard to accommodate me but it seemed the more they tried, the more I felt like a complete freak of nature. I do realise this is a very non politically correct way of putting it but I challenge anyone to find a better term. The problem with putting me in the new study area was that the staff there were used to trouble-making kids or students who needed more support with their learning. When I was there it was as if I was being babysat. I was spoken to like a small child and could have got more work done on my own, rather than getting simple tasks explained to me in great detail. I understand that this technique could work for some people but I was pretty smart and would have been better left to get on by myself.

Shortly after I somehow managed to avoid school again, which is when my auntie Mary suggested to my mum that I move to the North to live with my maternal grandparents. I would have full support from the family up there and Mary would get me all the help I needed with education. This meant I could complete my GCSEs at the school she worked at with my own age group. I instantly jumped at the idea and begged my mum to let me go. This kicked off a surprising amount of arguments though. My mum felt she could not let me go because she was my mother and it was her job to protect me. Mum's boyfriend decided I was just running away from my problems and I should grow up, stop attention seeking and just go back to school. He had been brought up believing that there was no such thing as depression, as it was just someone feeling sorry for themselves. He had no problem whatsoever voicing this opinion at home. He would make snide comments about me being a baby when I left a room, or pick fights with Mum about me getting a job if I was not going back to school;

'When I was her age... blah, blah, blah!' It was an absolute nightmare and I do not know how Mum put up with him.

One thing about break-ups is someone always gets hurt and a lot of spiteful things tend to be said or done which we normally would not dream of. Every Wednesday night my brother and I would go to our martial arts class and then have dinner at Dad's new house for a catch up. I do not think I tended to tell Dad a lot of what was happening at home because it would end up with nasty messages between him and Mum. He sent the RSPCA (Royal Society for the Prevention of Cruelty to Animals) to our house at one point, claiming that we were neglecting the dogs. I can only assume it was Mum who told Dad of the plans for me to move away; again, I cannot remember the details. I just know that a fuss was made about not trying every option. So I moved in with Dad and his new family.

They say opposites attract and this is definitely the case with my parents. My mum is very laid back and lets me and Ray make our own mistakes to learn from and will always support us no matter who we are or what we do. Obviously our dad loves us just as much but the reigns tend to be tighter at his end. I have never really been much of a girly girl and nine times out of ten will opt for a slouchy pair of ripped jeans and a hoody. This is not really suitable attire for a young lady in my dad's house though. So when I moved in with him, out went the band t-shirts and jeans and a whole new wardrobe was bought for me, even down to the underwear. New start: new clothes, new haircut and yes, you've guessed it, new school.

I was really excited about going back into education again and agreed to being dropped down a year. This was because my age group were apparently too far into their coursework and exam preparations for me to catch up. The school I was enrolled at was a rival school. I guessed that I would not know anyone, which meant the fact that I was a year older than my classmates would not matter. I settled into the routine pretty quickly. The syllabus for my chosen options was different to the previous school and so lessons were not too boring. Everything seemed easy until I started bumping into people that I knew from primary school or hobbies. In my previous school, the oldest two years had a different tie to the lower school but at this one it was only the Year 11s and so everyone's first response after asking what I was doing there was,
'Don't you have the wrong tie?'

I cannot remember why but the first time we had an assembly I got really overheated, my chest tightened and I felt like the room started to spin. I was taken outside to cool down and get myself together. I think it was either my form tutor or head of year who took me outside; whoever it was pulled me out of my first period lesson so she could keep an eye on me. Unfortunately the lesson she was teaching was a bottom set science lesson for my own age group and I loved every minute of it. The work was below my potential but after that, all I wanted was to be back in with my own peers; it was where I belonged.

The events of the next few weeks are a complete blur. At some point I think I was off school for a few days with chest pains from anxiety, but went to my martial arts session anyway with my brother Ray as usual. I knew I would be okay as I was aware of my limits and did not want to miss out on my martial arts. Towards the end of the first session though my dad turned up and pulled me out of the class. He had a massive go at me for going out when I was not well, and even though I told him it was from anxiety he was having none of it. I was given an ultimatum; go home with him that minute or pack my things and leave. I think a major thing to point out here is that while this 'discussion' was going on, the next group were waiting for their session to start, including Jamie. Dad always taught me to stick up for myself and I was in so much shock that I simply replied with, 'I will get my things tomorrow'. I went back into the hall, apologised to the teacher and was ushered out by two friends to find out what happened. As soon as we were in the changing rooms, I burst into floods of tears and told them what had happened between sobs. I cannot remember if we joined the class again after that or if I just sat out on the mats, but after the class Dad did not come to get us, so we had to ring Mum to come and pick us up. She was so confused and angry that Dad had just left us there.

I have no idea what happened in the days that followed. The next thing I recall is my Uncle John coming up from London to act as a voice for me during a meeting between me and my parents. All I can remember from it is Dad's girlfriend saying I was ungrateful and used their home as a hotel and Dad accusing me of only ever going back to my mum's for sex with random guys. Fantastic, cheers Dad! I have no idea what the end result was but somehow I ended up back at Mum's and owed Dad three hundred pounds for all the new clothes that he had bought. I think I only lasted a week or so after that at my new school before I dropped out because I had to walk passed the old one to get home.

It was May 2004 when I made the move to live with my maternal grandparents. Living with Mum did not last very long as her boyfriend had the new advantage that my own dad did not want me any more. Leaving my home town was a massive step but my grandparents were amazing and so supportive of the situation. It was too late to do my exams by this point and so we concentrated more on looking at College courses that would accept me without any qualifications. The local Art College is literally a five minute walk from my grandparent's house; so my uncle Andrew went with me to an Open Day. The letter at the beginning of this story was part of my application to join the GNVQ (General National Vocational Qualification) Art and Design Course there. I was successful in my application and went on to study there for three years which led to going to university.

It has been two years since I started to tell you my tale. Unfortunately I ended up dropping out of university after realising it was not for me. I went on to do a Teaching Assistant course with a placement in a secondary school. A lot of bad memories were triggered off from being in that environment. It just felt like I was back in the classroom as a student again. Not long after this I had one of my worst breakdowns to date. Although it was painful at the time, it has had a very positive effect on everything as it was the final push I required to convince my doctor that I needed to seek added professional help.

I still see a counsellor who agrees that writing my story to share with others is a very therapeutic way to reflect on my experiences. The fact that I am a lot older has meant I have been able to look at the past events with a better perspective. It took me a lot of years to get over the feeling that my mum chose her boyfriend over me, but now I know she was only doing what she thought was best for me at the time by letting me leave to live with her parents. I have a better relationship with my dad but do not get to see him as much as I would like and birthdays and Christmas times are always hard without him around.

I continue to take antidepressants to control my anxiety levels and rather than self-harming, I have started to turn the negative into the positive and get tattoos done instead; they are a much prettier way of suffering pain. Life is very hard sometimes but I have learnt it is the way you deal with it that makes the person. Sink or swim. Bring on the water...

Maggie Hodgson

Names have been changed by request

The Lord Does Not Disappoint

Bipolar is a chemical imbalance. Not unlike diabetes, it is controlled by medication. Saying this, why then is there a stigma? Is it my fault I am bipolar? Is there some truth still in the age-old association with evil spirits?

What is stigma? A 'not-in-my-backyard' complex? A reaction to 'strange behaviour' associated with a label? Do you realise then that 'strange behaviour' can be a minimal component in the lives of persons who are mentally ill, and yet one would label them for life?
What is the root of their illness? Could it be abuse? Neglect? Normal anxieties that have precipitated a breakdown?

Who tells me it is my fault now? Yes, mine was one of incest. An experience I was to begin as a young child. My fault? It lasted many years before I blurted it out to a sister. This, as a young seventeen-year-old. I left home.

My sister too had shared that experience, and with having two other sisters, I made a point of finding out whether they too had been abused. Prior to leaving home, I sensed my father's attention on my younger sister. I challenged him, warning him to leave her alone.

For a year or so, all was quiet. It was then that my mother discovered the truth. She was devastated. However, she remained faithful to my father.

I travelled overseas as an exchange teacher. This, for me, was a fresh start. On a return trip to the United Kingdom, I visited our fourth sister who lived abroad. It was a challenging but necessary task. We consoled each other as we were to realise the extent of my father's abuse.

In the early days, I had approached a priest to warn off my father. He did so, leaving myself and our youngest sister in my father's care.

The abuse did not stop. Indeed our father was now turning his attention to a niece.

It was in the early days of living abroad that I received a phone call from my younger sister. She was calling from a psychiatric hospital.

'I have bulimia. What am I to do?' Mum and Dad had been informed and were being counselled... 'But Dad will not talk.' I sent a friend to her side and arranged for her to join me at the earliest. This she did. We talked a great deal. Dad, it seemed, was behaving. The boys - all three of them - had met and decided not to prosecute. Home was a safe place. My sister was taking no chances. She was residing in a student flat. This illness, was it her fault?

Not long after, my brother brought his family over to immigrate. The arrangement was a bit of a squeeze. I fell ill. All sorts transpired and I was admitted to a psychiatric hospital. I was diagnosed with bipolar disorder. What do you expect? My fault? I challenge you with the question if only to examine your thoughts and attitudes towards persons with a mental illness. What lies behind the eyes of the one who presents the symptoms or has the label?

In time, I had to decide to come home. I needed to learn more about the illness and how to manage it. My teaching was not compromised. Fearful of returning to the 'home', I set up on my own. School was a challenge. Jobs were temporary to begin with... then made permanent. Before long, I was back in the Catholic sector, contributing to the school community.

Going through counselling was a decision I made. I did so at a Catholic Social Services Centre, and made great headway. At the same time I shared the content of all my visits, and advice given, with each of my sisters. It brought about a great peace.

Dad was still with us until a ripe old age. I loved my mum dearly and to be close by was to endure my father's role. I did not turn my back. Some people would say I was crazy. I set up home on the other side of the city and established myself both at school and in the local Church community.

Manic depression, as bipolar disorder was known then, had its own Fellowship. I joined a self-help group, attending on a regular basis before acting as Vice Chair of a local Community Mental Health Forum. This was to become an integral part of my life.

Form Community to the Church: I established a couple of self-help groups - these under the auspices of Our Lady of Mental Peace. This was a new title for Mary, first becoming known to me in the year 2000. It was then that I sparked off an investigation into its origin. It led, from the United Kingdom to Boston, Massachusetts, where I met with the founder, an elderly priest, Monsignor William Sullivan. We spoke of mental health and the Church, and this devotion that had been blessed by both Pope John XXIII and Pope Paul VI.

I returned to the United Kingdom with great enthusiasm and a desire to foster this new title for Mary among the ranks of those with a mental illness. However, the words of Our Lady's prayer do not identify mental illness alone, 'but what is essential in our weakness...' Alone, the prayer speaks to many more.

Before long, we were presenting Our Lady of Mental Peace to the Church community. The Archbishop lent his support. Conferences too were established in her honour, encouraging all aspects of mental ill health and the sharing of information and support, this, on an annual basis.

Monsignor Sullivan and I kept very much in touch, sharing the way forward. I was to return to Boston shortly before his passing in 2007. I am pleased to carry his spirit with me in the work that I do.

I now reside overseas, back to my earlier days, setting up anew. I am happy and life is fulfilling, each day a challenge of a different sort. A pleasurable challenge. It is to the Lord I look for guidance and strength. He does not disappoint.

Margaret

Writer's name has been changed by request

Empowerment

Some years ago I read an article in our monthly diocesan newspaper written by a student undergoing training to the priesthood. He had spent time gaining experience in a parish and wrote about how valuable and helpful it was for him. Although he recalled different sorts of ministry he had undertaken, there was no mention of people with mental illnesses and I wrote to him regarding this. He very courteously replied to me. Later, after his ordination, he was appointed to our parish to help our parish priest in ministry. I introduced myself and gave him a copy of my first published book. He accepted it graciously and told me that he would read it.

Months later I was discussing with this priest, Father Bill, of my desire to set up a pastoral support group for people in our communities who were experiencing mental ill health. It had been troubling me for some time that this seemed to be an area where there was possibly a gap in pastoral care in the community. Father Bill immediately offered to help me and with this encouragement, we together arranged to meet with two ladies whom I had come in contact with and who had expressed an interest in coming to a pastoral support group. We met fortnightly at first. Others joined and we all benefitted greatly from Father Bill's guidance, support and priestly ministry. Only when Father Bill was moved to the other side of the diocese did he cease to attend our pastoral support group. I am indebted to him for his care, guidance and spiritual nourishment as are those people who came to the meeting.

I asked Father Bill if he would write a few lines on this area of pastoral care and he sent me the following:

'Ideas are learnt through the media: negative, fear, violence. You learn with contact through people and I think you can be trained. For example, do not say 'pull yourself together'. There are basic rules, good guidelines, to walk with people with mental illness. Pastoral studies were very strong as I did a theology / ministry degree when training.

My first contact was when I was asked to visit a lad with schizophrenia and I was apprehensive as I did not know what I was going to face, but I thoroughly enjoyed visiting him and have done so, many times since.

I gained insights from groups and from the hospital, but more so in groups. More severe in hospital, but I am still learning from them and I learnt a great deal from them but they are a bit more defensive, but in groups they are more open. The best way to learn is to have contact with them and let them tell you and if they get angry, just let them, and if they want to talk about Church, let them. Empower the people in the groups; for example, what do you want, the decision is yours.'

Rev. Bill Serplus

Diocese of Middlesbrough

Mental Illness And Belief

Looking back, I realise that I have had a mental illness for as long as I can remember. My family thought of me as being moody and very bad-tempered. I had my first bout of serious depression when I was seventeen and at a Sixth-Form College. I became a different person, always very tired, stayed in bed for long periods of the day, and was often absent from College. I was very anti the music teacher whom I saw as being very arrogant and not good for my self-esteem; so I was often rude to him. I isolated myself at home by spending hours in my bedroom, easily upset, often angry and irritable, had difficulty in communicating, and when in the kitchen looked at the knives and thought how easy it would be to pick one up and kill myself; I also did the same with tablets.

Obviously I was extremely unhappy with myself, confused, and wanted to be helped but did not know how. It was clear to my parents that something was wrong and they kept questioning me.
'What is the matter? What is wrong?' My older brother, John, whom I was very close to, also asked because my parents thought that I was more likely to tell him. How could I when I myself did not know? They were very worried about me. Eventually Dad took me to see our doctor. My mother would not go as she said that Dad would be listened to, another indicator of how worried they were, as I usually went on my own and never with my dad. My doctor said that I was recovering from influenza even though I had not been ill.

A few months later when watching television, I saw a programme about depression and recognised myself and told my parents who had also watched the programme. However, we did not do anything about it as, by this time, I was beginning to pick up and I refused to talk about it for a very long time. I think I was ashamed of how I had been. Obviously, my College work suffered and I did not do as well as I should have done at my exams, but I managed to go on and qualify as a teacher.

Initially, it did not affect me spiritually, as thanks to my primary school and the nuns there, as well as my parents and my grandmother, I had a deep faith in God and constantly turned to Him and Mary for help and support. I spent a lot of time praying and I am certain that this is what kept me going over the years.

I was affected following my diagnosis of having a mental illness. Having been absent from work as a result of the illness, for several months at a time, I found that I could not continue to work and was allowed to retire on grounds of ill health. As a courtesy, I telephoned the head to inform her and was shocked at her response.
'Oh, you are ill then!' Not the expected response as I had worked closely with this person for several years.

My spiritual difficulties began during the year I was off work prior to retiring. During that year, apart from one occasion, none of my colleagues visited me. Several of them lived nearby. Apparently, when they saw Kevin, my husband, or my friend, Catherine, they asked after me. Both Kevin and Catherine said to call in or telephone me and not to worry because, if I did not feel up to the contact, I would say so. My ex-colleagues did not make the effort and it was as though I was a different Mary now that I had a mental illness. As I worked in a Roman Catholic primary school where we taught Christian values, this neglect was difficult to understand. As Christians, surely they should have been there for me?

I usually played the organ at Saturday evening Mass but was no longer able to. I contacted the clergy to let them know and said that when I well enough to play again, I would be in touch. I had been finding it difficult to attend Mass during that year because I felt unacceptable to members of the congregation. I knew that my body language discouraged people from approaching me. That was not what I wanted. I did not wish to have a conversation but would have appreciated a touch on my arm and a smile to reassure me that I was acceptable in spite of my illness. Not much to hope for, I thought. The whole of the Mass was a constant reminder to me that I was not experiencing the love, support and care that Jesus taught all of us to give. Selective Christianity! We will apply it to well-known members of the community and to those who have an obvious physical illness, but we will avoid those whom we find difficult to be with and those who have a mental illness. Regularly, during Mass, I had a very strong urge to stand up and shout out, 'What about me? Where do I fit in to all of this?' I stopped attending Mass. This upset my husband because he knew the importance of my faith to me, but he fully understood why I stopped going.

I was further hurt when the clergy did not visit me. There was obviously a problem. Eventually, I plucked up courage to ask Kevin if the clergy asked about me. It was not a surprise to hear the answer was 'no'. It was not as though I was a stranger to them. I needed not only support from my family, but also from my parish family. I felt so alone, and the neglect reinforced my low self-esteem and sense of worthlessness. At times I was very angry about my situation. It was difficult enough to have a mental illness without the added lack of spiritual and community support. I decided that I needed to deal with it. I approached a curate in the parish who was known to me as not only had he visited my classroom but I also spoke to him at the cathedral. On one occasion, I offered to speak with him about my experience of mental illness because I was confident that he would meet many like me, over the years. The offer was not taken up. My chat with him was very damaging to me and if anything, made matters worse. He kept saying the same thing to me:

'You only had to ask for help.' He could not understand that it is impossible to do that. It is very important to have the need recognised, and to be approached. It became apparent to me that I was upsetting him and I backed off. I kept apologising and left. There was no help or support given.

Some time later, I approached the bishop who was happy to talk, but said that awful phrase

'You have to make allowances. People do not understand.' I have a question. Why? Why do I have to make allowances? Are they frightened that I might suddenly turn on them and harm them physically? I am the one who is ill and in need of help.

Obviously, none of these experiences did anything to stop my resentment for my parish community. They fed it. Over time I recognised that I needed spiritual input as well as contact with my faith community. Having recognised this, I met with the bishop on several occasions and explained what I thought was needed for myself and others like me. He did not understand that I was not able to do this myself. I had the idea but it required others to put it in place. I gave up.

The only good thing to come out of the chats with the bishop was meeting Edna. Having given up, the support that I needed arose. It took years to arrive at this point and it was such a relief. I cannot recall how many years it took but our group was worth waiting for. The mix of spiritual input, sharing of our lives, and the social time that we have is very important to me. It is my only contact with my faith community as I still cannot attend Mass. I attend other churches now and again, but unfortunately my negative experience with my parish community has resulted in my feelings been transferred to all Roman Catholic communities.

How different it would have been had I had the experience of Christian love and caring that my husband received during his latter years with terminal cancer. He was very aware of the different treatment that he received from his colleagues (Kevin taught in a Roman Catholic secondary school), and also from our parish community and clergy. He had regular visits from his colleagues, from the chaplain and our parish curate. He was very hurt for me, and my observations of his good experience just fuelled my anger, hurt, and the feeling of being rejected / unwanted.

My experience makes it very clear that support is needed. All of the time, I have been aware of all those who have suffered in silence and needed support from their church. Perhaps they have left and nobody has noticed.

'You have to make allowances. People do not understand.' Therefore, parishioners need to be helped to understand; so some sort of education is required. They also need to know that they can help just by acknowledging a person with a nod or smile or touch or a combination. It is that easy. Do it to everybody and what a lot of good feeling will be generated. The clergy need to be educated as they often meet parishioners with a mental illness, but may avoid them because they can be very difficult to be with. I think that we are all aware of that.

For those who need more, then a pastoral support group like ours could be good for them, spiritual, mutually supportive and providing social occasions. There are support groups out there, but I felt strongly that the Church should be able to support its own and a good beginning is a group, as members begin with two things in common, mental illness and belief. Groups should be open to accepting a person who wants to become more involved in supporting those who need it. The clergy should visit a group from time to time even if they unable to make a commitment to regular meetings.

Bishops need to be pro-active and encourage support. I suppose education should begin with them. They in their turn should make sure that the clergy of the diocese should attend an awareness day where they will, hopefully, gain an understanding of what it is like living with mental illness, as a sufferer and as a carer. All of them need to be aware that support requires flexibility. There is no one right way. Support may be one to one at home by priest, deacon or sympathetic parishioner, being accompanied to Mass, or being part of a pastoral support group. I envisage there could be many of these. So it may be necessary for parishioners, able to empathise, to help establish a new group.

Mary

I So Much Want To Die

We had an inaugural Healing Mass before we initiated our first official pastoral support group for carers of people experiencing a mental illness. At this first meeting was a lady whom I had not previously met. Tall and slim, well spoken and exceedingly articulate, she shared her views over the months on the Scripture readings with apparent ease and certainly with knowledge but she did not push her views on others. They were her own insights that she gave in a quiet way and she left plenty of space for others to contribute. She told us nothing about herself but continued to come month after month for quite some time. Then one evening, the priest who was supporting us at each meeting told us that Kay was not coming any more as she felt that she did not fit in. Only then did I find out that Kay, single and retired from a professional occupation and an accomplished musician, experienced severe mental illness in her latter years and was still struggling with it.

I was troubled at the time to think that even though Kay had attended month after month that she was not comfortable in the group or apparently benefitting from participating. I felt that somehow we had let her down. However, Kay explained at a later date that, as carers, we share our ups and downs with regard to the person we look after but in Kay's situation it was different, as it was she herself who was struggling with her own depression, that we talked about our loved ones in the confidential non-judgemental setting but Kay did not have a loved one to talk about! It has been suggested to me at times that maybe the carers bring their loved ones with them but I have always felt this would not work and I feel that Kay illustrated this with her explanation as to why the support group was not beneficial to her.

I kept in touch with Kay over the years and we exchanged Christmas cards and the infrequent telephone call. She lives in a town further afield and I told her I was sending hugs down the line. She was lonely, alone with no family, and felt unable to talk about her depression and was disinclined to reveal it to her parishioners. She kept herself busy trying to help others by taking Holy Communion to sick people, giving individuals a lift to church or home, and playing the organ at Masses and other church services. She loves feeding the birds in her garden as she has a great love of the universe, the trees, flowers, birds and all living creatures and senses God's divine presence in the wonders of nature.

When I finally decided to initiate a pastoral support group for people in our communities with mental ill health, I thought about Kay. I telephoned her and explained about this different pastoral support group that I was beginning and invited her to come along. She declined and told me the reasons for her reluctance to join us.

'The trouble is I cannot encourage people, as life seems such a burden to me, just going on living. I so much want to die and be out of it. I start each day with a prayer and tell myself if God wants me to live another day then I will do the best I can. I have lost all faith in the Church. I believe others support me but it is blind faith. I go to Mass every week because I play the organ. I go in the week when a friend needs a lift or something, but again, I struggle with so much of what is done and said there. It makes so little sense in terms of the God I trust in and Jesus whose life I want to follow.'

We kept in touch and eventually Kay decided to 'give it a go' and come to one of our support meetings, the one specifically for those with mental ill health who are looking for some spiritual nourishment and support. Kay shared with us over the months her story.

'I first experienced depression when my mother died suddenly in January 1989. At the time I was teaching at a Sixth Form College. When she died, my life seemed very empty. After the funeral, I returned to school, but eventually I had to go to the doctor and was given some pills, but no time off. After developing bulimia and losing a lot of weight, I went into a mental hospital. A priest was very good and brought me Holy Communion every day until I was allowed to go out to Mass. I was very touched by this and he will probably never know how much this meant to me. After two months, I was discharged and was supposed to see a clinical psychologist but this never really happened as there were long waiting lists. I was made redundant in 1992 and felt very upset at the way it happened and the lack of any concern from the senior staff of what I had been led to believe was a caring Catholic community.

My best help came from a bereavement counsellor, whom I met at a Eucharistic ministers' meeting, who offered help. Although people can be sympathetic when they know you are suffering, I do not think that the church community knows how to help except for promising to pray, and I do not know how to ask.'

One of Kay's hobbies is making candles out of old scraps of candle wax. At Christmas, she brings each of us in the pastoral group a coloured candle. She takes great interest in the participants and is very compassionate towards others and their problems. It is not unusual to receive a telephone call from Kay enquiring after a group member or a member of one's family.

As she was leaving after one of the meetings, Kay commented on how lovely it was to be with people where she can truly be herself and not be judged. She has apparently built up enough trust to know that, when surrounded by friends in the support group, she has no need to wear a 'mask' and pretend everything is okay when it is not. She is accepted as she is. She concluded that,

'I think the groups you have set up sound marvellous, just to be with people without feeling a nuisance.'

Kay

Scared

Scared of life, scared of death
Scared of people I haven't met
Scared of love, scared of hate
Scared of hunger with nothing on the plate
Scared of me, scared of you
Scared of feeling that there's no way through
Scared of rain, scared of the sun
Scared of walking when there's nowhere to run

Scared of violence, scared of war
Scared of politics; what's it all for?
Scared of lies, scared of truth
Scared of the dentist extracting my tooth
Scared of darkness, scared of light
Scared of dogs with vicious bites
Scared of heaven, scared of hell
Scared of talking with nothing to tell

Scared of football, scared of the roar
Scared of my team when they fail to score
Scared of money, scared of being poor
Scared of thinking positive which makes me unsure
Scared of eviction, scared of feet
Scared of catching food poison from a mouldy piece of
meat
Scared of going up in a lift, scared of going down
Scared of voices saying 'oh look here comes the clown'

Scared of being noticed, scared of all those eyes
Scared of all the critics; being drunk's a good disguise
Scared of growing weaker, scared of growing wild
Scared of having thoughts around suicide
Scared of all the tears, scared they'll see me cry
Scared for all the daughters who lose the loving child
Scared of the future, scared of the past
Scared of the friendships which never seem to last

Scared of television, scared of the news
Scared of all those people with a different point of view
Scared of my girlfriend, scared that she'll leave
Scared of being alone with nothing to read
Scared of stealing, scared of being caught
Scared of being questioned about items I should have
bought
Scared of going places, scared of staying in
Scared of all the drunkards on the park bench with their
gin

Scared of heavy footsteps, sacred as they get closer
Scared of unfamiliar faces; 'sorry but I don't know ya'
Scared of heavy drinking, scared of being sober
Scared on the edge of a cliff; someone could push you
over
Scared of men in suits, scared of what they say
Scared of men in white coats coming to take me away
Scared of destruction, scared of blood
Scared of being scared and that's no good

Shaun Elliot, 1991

Shaun's friend tells me that Shaun is now in a healthy
place, in good shape and has a good full life. She adds
that people do recover from anxiety and illness and this
is a hopeful message to remember.

My Family Is The Family Of God

I offer this letter with my love to my family and to the extended family I have chosen for myself, the family of God. My family is the family of God. I love all my family without exception very much. My relationship with my family is very important to me. This letter is my love letter to you to say no matter what happens in life, I will always love you. You will always be in my thoughts and prayers. People from all walks of life may have injuries that no-one can see. Christ calls us to be compassionate to one another. I am sincerely sorry for any time I have hurt anyone, or my behaviour has been difficult for others to understand. I give all the hurts I have experienced and any hurt I have caused to God. I trust His love will do the rest.

I have some problems that have an effect on my health and ability and in some ways have hindered my relationship with the people I love, especially the people close to me. Love does not always run smoothly and life is often messy with not enough time for explanations or attention to details. I would like to shed some light on some of my difficulties as I perceive them. I have experienced the effects of mental ill health at intervals throughout my life. I account for my reluctance to seek help until recent years as being due to the social stigma of mental illness. In my mind, I am taking a risk in sharing my experience because in disclosing serious recurring problems of mental ill health, I feel vulnerable to what others may think of me. I have taken my example from the woman in the Bible who touched Jesus' cloak (Lk.8:43-48). Her illness of 'bleeding' at her time in history was socially unacceptable and is comparable with mental illness in today's society. She was afraid but she decided to get close to Jesus and touch Him regardless of the cost. The woman knew she would be healed if she could even touch Christ's garment, his cloak.

Physical or emotional trauma can trigger brain injury. Emotional trauma can have a similar effect as blows to the head. Informed professionals agree that clinical depression is a physical illness in the same way as measles or pneumonia are illnesses. The title of a book by Doctor Tim Cantopher (2006) is *Depressive Illness: The Curse of the Strong*. (Sheldon Press, SPCK). Too much pressure for too long and coping with pressure that many would run away from - conditions are created to blow a fuse...

When I am well, I would say I have good social and communication skills. My skills desert me when I am sick. I find it hard to put words together. My thoughts come either very quickly or very slowly. I cannot retain information or co-ordinate simple tasks effectively. I get in a mess. I become easily confused, anxious and highly sensitive to noise. It is as if a thick heavy fog descends on my mind and body. I cannot understand or describe some of the states I find myself in; they seem to come from thin air, though exhaustion and prolonged stress are usually factors. To put it simply, my brain and my speech do not behave in the way I expect them to work. This is very unsettling and causes me to feel at times like I am drowning in fear. Under pressure of severe symptoms, confusion and distress, at times I have not made a very good job of communicating in recent years. As a result, there have been many misunderstandings between others and myself. I am sorry for my part in any misunderstandings. The continued effort needed to survive this complex illness is at times exhausting.

I am a responsible adult, mother and grandmother, retired nurse and local government community development worker. I have seen and experienced my fair share of suffering of many kinds. For me and many others, the physical and emotional suffering of mental illness is the worst kind imaginable. Death can look like a desirable option at times. I came close to taking my own life some years ago following a long illness of anaemia, injuries and brain chemical imbalance that became unbearable. Thanks to God I have a wonderful family, though I felt I was a burden to my husband and children. My thoughts in illness and weakness began to turn towards death as a means of relief from torment and pain. I felt useless and worthless. Some thoughts during mental illness are not logical or a true reflection of reality. Suicidal thoughts are not uncommon but most people do not act on these thoughts and feelings of despair.

Then one day I moved from thinking about ending my life to taking some actions in that direction. I prepared to take some tablets to end the unbearable suffering, believing wrongly it would be the best thing for everyone if I were not here to bother them with my illness and its effects on them, the people I loved. After taking tablets out of the cupboard, part of my mind realised that this was a bad idea and I put them away. This behaviour continued as I had a mental and spiritual battle of going to the edge and then backing away. The tablets were in and out of the cupboard. Repeatedly I prayed to my guardian angel and I called on my family in heaven to help me. I went to the phone and called the Pastoral Centre. A Catholic priest answered my call for help. I told him what was happening. He told me God was with me always. He prayed with me on the phone. He said God would not leave me. I knew what the priest said was true. I just needed someone to remind me of the truth. Brain chemical dysfunction caused me almost to forget that I had choices and for a while I could see only one option. I was so afraid of my thoughts and possible actions. I went outside to wait and to make space between the tablets and myself... The priest came by taxi and he gave me the Sacrament of the Sick. He waited with me until my husband came home from work. The priest acted beyond my expectations and through his love and care helped to direct me back on the road to health. The priest advised me to ask for help from my doctor, which I did. I have very good doctors who have given me help and care.

I have had personal relationships with seven people who have taken their own lives when unbalanced by mental illness. These people were my brothers and sisters in Jesus Christ and I love each one of them. They lost their grip on valuable life when ill and vulnerable. Authentic love does not die. The love of God extends beyond physical life.

I began writing this letter a few months ago on the feast of Pentecost. I rely on my faith in God for my survival as my faith in God is my medicine and my armour. I am alive today only by God's grace. The Holy Spirit was the first gift to us from Jesus Christ after His Resurrection. Jesus sent the Holy Spirit for everyone, not for a select few. <u>The Holy Spirit comes to help us in our weakness</u> (Ro.8:26). The Holy Spirit is my comforter and helper.

I make use of any means I find helpful to stay as well as I can. I have developed many ways of managing the health challenges I experience and because at times brain chemical dysfunction causes problems for me and seriously affects my senses, I need to give myself a lot of reminders of healthy actions to take when necessary. I have had training in mental health first aid that I found really helpful in managing my condition. The training is also helpful for supporting other people. I have had very good doctors and I request psychiatric help when I need it.

For me the sacraments of the Catholic faith and our family Bible have been the essentials of my life but God's love extends beyond the sacraments. Thomas Aquinas insisted God is not limited in his gift giving to those who are sacramentally united with Him. Faith is the opposite of fear and faith comes from hearing God's Word. In Luke's Gospel (Lk.8:43-48), there was a woman in the Bible days who was sick for a very long time. When she heard Jesus was passing by, she pushed her way through the crowd and she reached out and touched him. The woman had faith and hope in her heart. Jesus said to the woman,
'Your faith has saved you.' This passage has meaning for me and reminds me of what I need to do at times when I am sick or in distress. The name of Jesus is a strong tower for me, a strong motivation to health, life and love. My medicine is the name of Jesus. His name causes healing and gives rest to my mind and body. Speaking his name with my lips or speaking his name silently in my heart, his name calms me and helps me to choose life. His name brings light into the darkness. Health and wholeness for me means knowing that God is with me and understands what I do not understand. When I cannot pray myself, I rely on the prayers of other people. I thank God for my health.

This prayer serves as another reminder for me because when I am sick I can sometimes forget that I have faith... I can sometimes think that God does not exist.

Refuse To Fall Down

CP Estés (1995) The Faithful Gardener: A Wise Tale About That Which Can Never Die. Harper, San Francisco

If you cannot refuse to fall down, refuse to stay down
If you cannot refuse to stay down, lift your heart toward heaven
And like a hungry beggar, ask that it be filled
You may be pushed down. You may be kept from rising
But no one can keep you from lifting your heart toward heaven
Only you
It is in the middle of misery that so much becomes clear
The one who says nothing good came of this
Is not yet listening

St Paul discusses in his writing what he calls 'a thorn in the flesh'. It is not clear exactly what it was. Three times he prayed for it to be taken away but was told,

My grace is sufficient for you because my power is made perfect in weakness (2Co.12:9)

We do not know what thorns life has in store for any of us. We are not promised life free from pain or difficulties but active faith in God will give us the strength to cope with whatever comes to us. Christ's garments touched the earth and they got messy and dirty in his service to us. The garments of Jesus Christ represent God's love on earth. We are all called to the service of love. When we love, God acts. My family is the family of God. There is no hurt that God cannot heal with his love.
Let us love one another, for love is from God. Whoever loves is a child of God and knows God (1Jn.4:7)

Edna Hunneysett

Together We Helped To Build An Ark, A Place Of Safety

How was it done? When it was suggested to me that I might benefit from joining a mental health support group in the diocese, my first reaction was the thought thank you but no thank you. I had experienced a recurrence of clinical depression and anxiety, a condition with similar features of other mental illnesses including: exhaustion, feelings of isolation, thoughts like 'I don't want to die but I have no energy to function, breathe, think, or live...' I thought to myself, the last thing I needed was the company of people who felt like I did. I feared this would make me feel more ill and depressed. I imagined a group of people focused on problems and illness and I certainly did not want to be part of a group like that. I told my kind friend, I will let you know. In time, after feeling a bit more lost and desperate, I decided to give the group a try and I thank God that I did because I have discovered a place of refuge, strength, grace and healing.

For where two or three meet in my name, I am there among them (Mt.18:20)

Why does the group work? The group works because we believe and experience the Holy Spirit, who is invited and present with us. How? There is a high level of trust amongst the participants that has developed through time spent in prayer, meditation on the Word of God from the Scriptures and sharing of individual experiences without fear of negative judgements or criticism. Could the group develop? Yes. We want to share what we have discovered in the hope and belief that other small groups could come together using a simple format 'K I S S' 'Keep it Safe and Simple'.

Safe: even among some Christians, there is a stigma of mental ill health and some of us feel we do not want to be identified as attending 'a support group' unless we decide to make a self-disclosure if and when appropriate. Within the group, confidentiality is an essential element of our relationship. The sharing together of heart, mind and spirit must be within a safe place, without fear of personal or family information being discussed outside of the group, and the sacred space created by God's presence within. We have had up to eight people in the group and this number is flexible. We all feel that small is easier to cope with, in allowing each person to feel at ease and able to speak if they want to do so. There is no pressure to talk. Each person is giving a valuable contribution by being 'present'. Quietness or silence is perfectly acceptable.

Simple: an opening prayer is offered. We open in prayer remembering we belong to God's family and He is present with us. We share each other's company and tasty tea and cake. We share a Scripture reading and meditation. These can be found on www.rc.net/readings/index.html Following reflections, a closing prayer is offered with thanks to God for all we have received in our encounter with Him and each other. The meeting lasts for one hour and thirty minutes.

What are the benefits? Each person in the group has reported positive health effects of our time together in mutual giving, sharing and receiving, within a God-centred environment. Together we thank all who have made this group possible. My personal benefits: I reluctantly left a career I enjoyed, ten years ago, following a long and complex illness of severe anaemia. (Mental illness often accompanies physical ill health). Thanks to this wonderful group of people, I am no longer ashamed that sometimes I get sick because I realise I am how God created me for His purpose. When I have health and energy, I work therapeutically and creatively in ways that are meaningful to me. The rainbow is my favourite symbol from the Bible, signifying joy, hope and love. Creativity is an integral part of our humanity and a gift of the Holy Spirit of God. I enjoy writing, singing and playing with my beloved grandchildren. The group has helped me to develop a greater attitude of gratitude.

...your light must shine in people's sight, so that seeing your good works, they may give praise to your Father in heaven (Mt.5:16)

After meeting regularly for five years, we named this project Ark. Ark is a place of safety. Ark is a resource developed in the diocese of Middlesbrough for people living with mental health challenges. A person attending this group may be living with mental illness, recovering from mental illness, managing a condition or recovered from mental illness. It is a misconception that people with mental illness cannot get better. Ark provides opportunity for prayer, care, acceptance, learning, growth and health improvement. It also provides resources beyond the group through links with local and national initiatives.

Some Suggestions

- ✓ Enrol on a two day Mental Health First Aid course (mhfa England).
- ✓ The MIND charity runs a two day training course in Mental Health First Aid.
- ✓ Read Edna Hunneysett's books: *Our Suicidal Teenagers: Where are you God?* and *Pastoral Care Mental Health.*
- ✓ Set up Ark groups pioneered for six years by Edna Hunneysett in Middlesbrough. The

pastoral mental health support group pioneered by Edna has been for me like spiritual first aid and I would recommend its format to other pastoral groups.

✓ Church: All Holy People of God. Help those in need to reach out and touch the hem of Christ's garment: the sacraments.

✓ Holy Catholic Church: please do not be stingy with the sacraments; they belong to us. We need them. I have been to a church service where only physically sick people were invited to receive the Sacrament of the Sick.

✓ Due to shortage of priests, train special ministers of mental health to administer Sacraments of the Sick and Eucharist to those with mental illness.

✓ Church: train priests and nuns and lay ministers to give help to people who are ill mentally and to be on call for times of crisis.

✓ Keep a personal mental health first-aid kit. Mine includes telephone numbers of health care professionals, doctors, counsellors and the Samaritans.

✓ Promote justice and peace of being accepted for people who are mentally ill.

Conclusion

When a mother gets sick, it has consequences for all of the family. I would like to thank all of my family for their love and patience with me, especially my husband Samuel (means 'sent from God', and he was). Sam has upheld me and loved me when I could not love myself or stand on my own feet. I thank God that despite many periods of illness, I have more than my share of happiness through the deep love I receive from God, my family and my friends which includes my new friends in the pastoral support group. For this I am always grateful.

Our Lady of Mental Peace, pray for us.

Choose Life

I have spoken about suicide and want to reassure anyone who knows and loves me that it is my firm intention to choose life for the rest of my life. I am confident that God has equipped me for life in Him. I have shared my experiences because of love.

The name of Jesus means God saves. God never stops saving. Even death cannot stop God from saving. After the name of Jesus, the two sounds that are imprinted on my heart, mind, soul and spirit are 'Choose Life' (Dt.30:19).

The Name Of Jesus

I am moved by obedience to Him
And writing here is not a whim
My family need not be alarmed
Because of Jesus, we'll not be harmed

For my friends who died before
I pray Jesus, hear, I love them more

The name of Jesus means God saves
And for us we will ne'er be slaves
I have a sound that rings in my ears
It's the sound of Jesus calming my fears

Catherine Marshall

Jesus Crowned With Thorns

Dear Jesus,

When I first began to gaze on You on the cross wearing the Crown of Thorns, I cannot pretend that I was not frightened. It seemed to me that after all the scourging You endured, this being crowned with twisted, dirty thorns by the Roman soldiers was just the ultimate in gratuitous violence and anger.

As time progressed, I came to see that this Crown of Thorns that pierced Your scalp, and even Your skull, was actually very necessary to visibly demonstrate Your total union with me and with others who experience depression and many other forms of mental illness. For love of us, Your sacred head, even when crowned, was beaten about with sticks and human fists.

You were thought to be completely mad because Your Love transcended rules and regulations that were rooted in fear and discrimination. So many jeered that You were the author of your own suffering and so 'really deserved all you got' - this is so often said to us.

As I prayed and came to make Your Head, Crowned with Thorns, the kernel of my spirituality, I came to realise that these Thorns created 'holes,' 'openings' and 'pathways' from Your mind to ours, by which the light of Your way of thinking could reach out to us and anoint our darknesses. In this sense, Your Crown of Thorns is purposeful, glorious and an invitation to us.

In our experience of mental distress, please help us to let You suffer in, with and through us. In Your great love and power, I believe that such suffering can be made valuable and 'enabling,' even though it might always remain mysterious - challenging us to trust You, the most innocent and greatest of Lovers, in a radical fashion. Amen

I have found that trying to focus on the psychological sufferings of Jesus and how He identifies Himself completely with me and my experience of mental sufferings not only fills me with gratitude, but also reminds me of how much I am loved and valued.

Maggie Quinn

Thorns created holes, openings and pathways from Your mind to ours, by which the light of Your way of thinking could reach out to anoint our darkness.

Your Crown of Thorns is purposeful, glorious and an invitation to us.

Jesus Crowned With Thorns

Where Is God In All This?

I was waiting to be introduced in order to give my talk at a Conference a few years ago and was watching as people arrived, some hesitantly and on their own whilst others came in pairs. A young lady and a man friend with her entered the room and were welcomed by one of the organisers and invited to have a cup of tea and take a seat. I wandered across to speak to them. The lady looked ill and the gentleman was protective of her. At the end of the conference, the young lady introduced herself to me as Jo and her friend told me his name was Frank.

'Jo is not well today,' he said.

'I can see that,' I replied and we talked quietly together, Frank and me, whilst Jo stood silently beside us. I gave them each a prayer card.

A year later, I was invited to speak at another Conference in that same diocese. Waiting and watching again, I saw Frank and Jo appear and one of the organisers brought them to me.

'I think these two are friends of yours,' she said. I struggled to remember their names, having only met them the once, and had to be reminded although I easily recognised their faces from a year ago. Jo looked even worse this time.

'She is really struggling today,' said Frank, 'but we saw the Conference advertised with you as speaker and we so much wanted to come again and hear you even though it is quite a distance for us to travel.' Jo found it difficult to sit through my talk and went outside to compose herself. She was ill.

At the end of the Conference I explained to Jo and Frank that I normally bring my books with me, that I had ordered a quantity to be sent directly from the publishers to the house of another friend as he and his wife were intending to come (they were to bring the books in their car and this saves me carrying them on my train journey). At the last moment, due to unforeseen circumstances, they did not make the Conference and my books were sitting many miles away in their home! I had arranged to speak the following day at the parish Masses whilst in the area but now would have no books to sell to those people who are interested in learning more about mental ill health and pastoral care.

'Tell me the address of your friend,' said Frank, 'and I will pick them up tonight and bring them to you in time for the first Mass tomorrow.'

'But it is miles away and a long return journey for you,' I replied.

'That's okay, 'said Frank. 'I do not mind doing this.' Both he and Jo came the next day with my books and stayed for the morning Masses. I meet wonderful people on my travels and amongst them, Jo and Frank are very special. I have not seen either of them since then, but we have corresponded intermittently.

When I informed Jo about collecting stories for my third book, she said she would write her story and send it to me. It is below.

'People who suffer any mental illness try to be creative in expressing what it feels like to go through it. This creativity has permeated into literature, art and music. Yet the cruel irony in this exercise for me is... if I had a pound coin for every time I hit the 'delete' button whilst writing this, to be sure there would be no need for me to buy any more lottery tickets!

As illness, mental and physical, has been in my family for many years, I would say that it is like a corkscrew twisted tightly into the soul. An invisible sticky dense cloud that takes forever to disperse before it comes back again. The pain of hopelessness. The ache of despair. The drought of time, empathy and understanding from those whom you would think might have even the slightest idea - they do not. The feeling of worthlessness overwhelms you. You feel guilty for breathing air.

There has been both mental and physical illness in my family. It has never been a case of going through a phase of illness and then moving on with our lives, like most people appear to be able to do. Lucky them!

Then my sister and I became chronically ill, physically and mentally.

Mental illness does not show any outward signs, apart from when you do not feel that there is any reason to smile. When you feel rotten, you attract insensitive remarks such as: 'Cheer up, it might never happen,' or else they mistake you for a pair of curtains: 'Pull yourself together!' It is far too easy to fall into the temptation of ending your life, which is a drastic way to kill the pain but you end up killing the rest of you. Believe me. I have been close to the edge. I still have those thoughts and they vary in strength.

Faith in God and His Holy Mother has been there for me like a gentle hand in my shirt collar, pulling me back from the brink with a brisk tug.

Having said that, it is understandable for anyone going through mental illness to ask the question: Where is God in all this? I have asked myself this question many, many times in my life.

The answer developed over the years – especially during Lent, Holy Week and Good Friday. Then there is Easter. Christ is on the Cross, sharing in your suffering. Popular prayers written about Christ's Passion are devoted to the Five Wounds (we all know that Jesus suffered more wounds than that) - His hands, His feet, His side. There is a sixth grievous 'wound' sub-divided into many, many wounds as Jesus also wore a Crown of Thorns on his head. Those thorns piercing into His skull, hammering into His skull each time the Cross nudges violently into the side of His Head on the way to Calvary. The mental anguish. The torment. The excruciating and unrelenting pain.

If no-one else understands where you are coming from when the black clouds start hanging over you like a bad smell, then Christ does. When your mind goes distorted like a short wave radio being tuned, it is hard to string your words or your prayers together. When all else fails, repeating this prayer over and over helps:

Jesus, mercy! Mary, help!

I sent an email to Jo to thank her for this write-up. I only realised just how tough she had found it, in her effort to put words to paper, when she responded to my thank you. She said,
'It is the hardest thing I have ever written and the procrastination in getting things down was due to the frustration as to where to start and to periods of depression as my depressive episodes have been pretty frequent of late. I did not know where to begin and so I prayed to Our Lord and His Holy Mother to help me make a start. Writing it has been more difficult than even I anticipated and it is great to let it go. May I wish you every success with your books - especially this one. If it helps in any way for whoever reads it or saves a life (because mental illness can be fatal if left untreated), it is God's grace and goodness at work through His instruments: ourselves.

Our Lady of Knock, comfort me when I am sick, lonely or depressed...

Jo

A Bipolar Experience

I was given this opportunity to tell my story. I decided that it might be therapeutic for me to do so. Others who are going through similar experiences, or have friends and relatives who are, may gain some benefit from reading this. In summary, I was diagnosed with bipolar at the age of forty-two after having two manic episodes that resulted in hospitalisation at the ages of twenty-five and forty. I have only had these two manic episodes. I have not yet suffered from depression.

Here Are The Details

I believe that Western society has an obsession with categorising everything and everyone. I do not think this has to do with wanting to 'control', more wanting to 'understand'. The result of this obsession is that people are constantly being put into boxes. What this ultimately results in are boxed-up people. We are so obsessed with needing to understand that we do not see the results that this causes.

I spent the first twenty-five years of my life feeling like a round peg in a square hole. I always felt that I did not fit and that some day somebody official would come along with a clip board and say, 'You are a mistake. You should not be here.' I certainly felt like I was a mistake. I felt like I was not in the right boxes. I was very introverted and very uncomfortable socially. I always considered others to be more important than myself. In fact, I considered myself to be insignificant.

So what happened when I was twenty-five that changed me? Well, I was at a point in my life where I had done a degree and was working in a decent job that I enjoyed. I was also spending most of my spare time in prayer. I would get in from work, cook a meal, clear up, then take to my bedroom with my Bible and religious books and spend hours reading and reflecting. My prayer life changed drastically. I confronted God and asked what it was that I was supposed to do with my life. I considered at the time that I could have a vocation. There was already a story in the family of how, when I was not yet at school, the local priest came round to the house for tea and asked me what I was going to be when I grew up. I answered, 'the Pope'. He laughed at this and informed me that only men could be Popes. My response was that I would be a priest. When I was then informed that priests could only be men, I somewhat irritatingly asked what it was that I could actually be. He responded with:

'A nun.' I replied, 'okay, I will be a nun then'. The only thing is I think something inside me still wanted and wants to be the Pope.

And so it was that night after night I sat on the floor in my bedroom. Eventually I looked closely at my faith in order to determine what the key messages were for me and the philosophy I wanted to adopt in living my life. I came up with the following list:

1) Love God with all your heart, mind and soul.
2) Love your neighbour as yourself (as each and every individual is unique, loved unconditionally by God and capable of totally amazing things).
3) Submit yourself totally to God.

I figured this would be enough to start with. I did feel that I was not too bad on the first and third items on the list but was pretty poor on the second. I did not treat my neighbour that well, but it was probably better than how I treated myself. It felt a little strange that the place I decided needed the most attention was actually my love of myself. I decided I would go along with it for a while at least and see how things went. I said to God that if I was loved unconditionally, then why did I not feel it? Why did I not actually feel loved or even lovable? This is when my prayer changed. I started to practice unconditional love meditations: hugging, bathing, breathing, and going atomic. These were all the different methods of mediation on unconditional love awareness that I devised and practised. After some weeks of this, I was getting rather good at it and I no longer felt unloved or unlovable. I felt transformed. I had so much energy. Everything and everyone looked different. I had some very usual experiences.

One that occurred quite often was the feeling of connectedness. It was as if every atom in every universe was somehow connected. My atoms were part of this. At these times, everything was complete. Everything was connected. Everything was also somehow equal. I still have this experience on occasions. Another experience I had that only happened once was one morning on the bus to work I saw the faces of my fellow passengers in total ecstasy. I knew that what I was seeing was not their actual faces but the joy of their souls knowing that they are unconditionally loved by God. I felt strongly at this point that I had a message for the Church and for the world. I did not know who to tell, how to tell it or even what the message was. I thought that I had a message. I told God that I was a willing servant and that I was prepared to go wherever I needed to be and do whatever I needed to do.

I had slipped on a tiled floor a few weeks before and banged the back of my head. I was having strange sensations and tasted blood when I went to bed and tried to sleep. I was rather concerned about what was happening. Eventually my GP referred me for a brain scan. When I got there I refused to put my head into the scanner as it looked like a giant tumble dryer. I was given an injection to put me to sleep and the next five days in hospital were something of a haze. I do remember haunting the nurse's station at three in the morning wearing my bottle-green dressing gown with the hood up. After a visit from a psychiatrist, I was moved into a mental health hospital as a voluntary in-patient, nowhere near a convent or religious order that I was expecting would be my place in God's plan. This was something of a shock. I did not think there was anything wrong with me. Everyone else was telling me that there was as, when I was given the sedative, I did not go to sleep as I was supposed to. I could not remember any of this.

And so it was that at the age of twenty-five, I was taken from a General Hospital to a mental health Assessment Unit (demolished some years ago). On arriving, the doctor who came to assess me, started by asking me why I had attempted to commit suicide. I burst into tears at this point. He asked me why I was crying. I informed him that I had not realised that I had attempted to commit suicide and that I was very concerned that I had done this and was not even aware of it. It turned out that I had not attempted to commit suicide. He just assumed I had. He had not bothered to look at my notes at all before talking to me. Probably not the best start to a doctor / patient relationship. It was not long before my doctor was changed. The next one was a lot better. I was in the mental health Assessment Unit for around eight weeks in total. After four weeks they thought I was ready to be discharged and informed me of this just prior to sending me home for the weekend. This was great news as I hated being at the hospital and now I was going to be free again.

When I returned to hospital on the Sunday evening, I was back to where I was when I was admitted.

Speeding! It was another four weeks before I slowed down again.

The First Discharge

I am to be discharged. I am going to be freed. I never wanted to be here. It was what I was told was best for me. I went along with it. If I did not, they might just make me anyway and so there was no point resisting. I just had to accept that they knew best. I never liked it here. It is an awful place. It smells awful. It looks awful. The sounds are awful. Just being here would make any sane person mad. It is a good job I am not sane.

I want to be somewhere calmer. Now I can be. I get my medication, eventually. I leave and go home. I feel totally different from when I was admitted. When I was admitted I was feeling positive. More positive than I have ever felt before. The racing thoughts were a nuisance. I did not like them. They have stopped now. I am not speeding any more. I was speeding for six weeks before I was admitted. It has stopped now. This is all in the past now. I am leaving. I feel very fragile now. Like a fresh egg. I feel like I can easily break. When I was actually released, I was really concerned that I could go high again as soon as I was discharged. I was not allocated any out-patient appointments or support. I was terrified. When I was feeling vulnerable, fragile and extremely confused, I was released from hospital. I did not understand what had happened, what was going on. What if I went high again?

After a few days, I phone the hospital and tell them that something is wrong. I am allocated an appointment with a nurse. His first question to me was why was I attention-seeking? I told him that I was not seeking attention, I was seeking support. Spending eight weeks locked up in an Assessment Unit and then to be cast out without any support to help me integrate back into society did not feel right to me. He asks me what is different about how I feel now and how I felt when I came in. I answer his questions. Even though I find his manner very flippant and condescending I remain calm with him. He could be doing it on purpose to see how I react. I think they do things like that sometimes. He decides that what I need is some support with my discharge. He arranges for me to see my psychiatrist as an outpatient. I have my support set up and so I leave. I was then allocated regular outpatient appointments with the doctor who had looked after me as an inmate. I was an outpatient for around two years. Much to my relief, his eventual diagnosis, from what I remember, was that my head injury had caused abnormal activity and he thought that that would be it. I was not really mad.

I still had my job and a few months after being discharged, I went back to work. I found it difficult to practice my faith and attend Mass. I still practised the unconditional love meditations and felt loved and lovable. I could not bring myself to do much else. I informed my father that I was getting some strong thoughts and feelings and that I was thinking of documenting them. He advised me against this. I respected his judgement and so did as he suggested.

I did not become a nun. I got married and had a family. When the children were small, I found my way back to my faith and started attending church again. I also eventually changed my employer. All appeared to be calm and ordinary again until I went to hear a Catholic priest give a talk. I spoke to him afterwards and mentioned something of the thoughts that I had and how difficult it was not to document them. He informed me that he thought that I should be documenting them.

This released a flood of thoughts for the following week or so. I kept waking up around two or three o'clock in the morning with my head swimming. The only way to make them go away was to write them down. My husband was not impressed with all this nocturnal activity. I tried to be discreet but he often caught me at it and voiced his displeasure. What was I supposed to do? Lie in bed with my head buzzing away waiting for morning to come?

The situation at work became difficult at the same time. I was caught up on the periphery of some inappropriate senior and middle management behaviour. The result of this was that a colleague and I had a very large amount of extra work dumped on us at the last minute. With my lack of sleep and the extra pressure at work, I started suffering from anxiety attacks. I went to my GP. He prescribed a wonder drug, Prozac. I was able to go back to work and managed to carry on with my life. Then one day a few weeks later, after visiting my GP on the way to work, I was in a one-to-one meeting with the assistant director. She stopped the meeting and informed me that I was ill and needed medical attention. She called in the Head of Human Resources and they arranged for me to go home. My husband managed to arrange for me to be seen by a doctor. I later found out from my GP that he realised that morning that I was in a manic state when I had seen him. He just did nothing about it. Mania is apparently a possible side affect of Prozac, so no harm there then.

The Second Admission

My thoughts are racing. They are going in every direction all at once. My head is spinning. My senses are heightened. Smell. Sight. Hearing. They are all working overtime. So many thoughts. I am not even thinking. They are just flowing. I do not know where they come from. I do not know how to control them. They are flooding my brain. My mind is drowning in them. I cannot breathe. They are overwhelming. My mind is drowning. I wish I could stop them. I wish I could divert them from my mind. I wish I could switch them off. My mind is drowning. I am drowning. I am not in control. I feel overwhelmed. I wish somebody would help me. I want somebody to switch them off. I want somebody to take them away. How can I have so many thoughts all at once? Where do they come from? How can I stop them?

My sleeping pattern was now widely disrupted. I only slept about two hours a night. I was getting higher. Eventually my husband had had enough and was unable to cope any more. He called out a doctor. The doctor comes to the house. He prescribes me a tablet. It is late. This will stop my thoughts. This will rescue my drowning mind. I take the tablet. The doctor's son is in a show that is taking place just around the corner. It is due to finish soon and he needs to pick him up. The doctor stays to talk to my husband until it is time for his son to be collected. I go to bed. I lie down and relax. I know the thoughts are going to go now. I know my mind is going to be rescued.

A few hours later I wake up. The thoughts are still racing. They have not stopped. They are actually worse. Something is not right. My husband makes more calls. It is about 2am and my head is swimming. My husband is instructed to take me straight to hospital.

They are going to admit me. We arrive at the hospital. My smell, hearing and sight are working overtime. I notice all the notices that are on the walls. I notice all the different smells as we walk through from the reception area to the ward I am to be admitted onto. I notice the sounds our different shoes make on the different types of floor we have to walk across. We wait for the duty doctor to arrive to admit me. There is so much going on. So many new sights, smells and noises. My thoughts are feeding on it. They are getting worse. The doctor comes. We talk. I am to be admitted.

My husband leaves. I get told which room I am to use. Round the corner first on the right. I am not escorted to the room. I am left to go on my own. I get round the corner. I see a man sitting on a chair in the corridor directly across from the room I have been allocated. He is alone. He looks at me. He has bad bruising on his face. He looks very unhappy. I feel frightened of him. I know nothing about him. I was really unnerved. There were no staff about and this guy was sitting just outside what was now my bedroom. I go into my room and close the door. There is no lock. I get into bed with my clothes on because I know there is a strange man sitting just outside my bedroom door. I was terrified and went to sleep terrified. Holding the blankets up to my face. It is 1999 and I am forty years old. I have just been admitted into a mental health hospital for the second time.

I was in hospital for around four weeks and was discharged just in time for Christmas. After a few weeks my medication started to be reduced. On Valentines Day, two weeks after my medication stopped and was out of my system, I went high again and had to be readmitted to the mental hospital. I was absolutely devastated. It was awful having to go back. My consultant now was a locum who had just come over from Australia for a year. He was still my consultant two years later when he informed me at my out-patient appointment that I was bipolar. I could not believe it. I did not want to believe it. I told myself that I was not bipolar.

The Diagnosis

Red. It is my favourite colour. It has been my favourite colour for as long as I can remember. Why do I like red? Red makes me feel energetic. Red makes me feel alive. My next favourite colour is black. Those who know these sorts of things inform me that black is not really a colour. It is actually the absence of all colours. Okay, that applies to light. If you have no light, it is black. I am not talking about light. I am talking about shoes. I am talking about coats. I am talking about little black dresses. I am talking about jewellery. Next to red I still like black best. Even if it is not a real colour. Why do I like black? Black is sophisticated. Black is classy. Red and black as a combination go really well together. I would like to feel this red and black. Sophisticated, classy, energetic and alive.

At the moment I am feeling red and black. It is not a sophisticated, classy, energetic and alive red and black I am feeling. I am feeling angry. More angry than I have ever felt before. The black is no longer the black of sophistication and class. It is the black of doom and gloom. The black of despair. The red is the red of rage. A rage so strong I feel like I am going to burst. Every cell is angry. More than that. Every atom is angry. I have just been informed, in the year of 2001 at the age of forty-two, that I have bipolar disorder. How could they have got it so wrong? How could I possibly have a mental health condition? These people must be utter fools.

This was me, some years ago now. The anger stayed for weeks if not months. I was so staggered at being told that I was bipolar that I froze. I wanted to say 'No, you must be wrong', or 'What on earth has made you come to such a decision?' I do not say anything. I freeze. For weeks, or possibly months, I live with the anger. Getting up with it. Having breakfast with it. Brushing my teeth with it. Going to work with it. Doing my work with it. Having lunch with it. Coming home with it. Having tea with it. Cleaning the house with it. Shopping with it. Going to bed with it. Breathing in with it. Breathing out with it. I thought the anger was never going to go away. How could it? They were so wrong. No way did I have a mental health condition. People with mental health conditions were freaks. Weren't they?

I did not know anyone with a mental health condition. Did I? I had seen people with mental health conditions. People walking the streets looking unkempt and mumbling to themselves. I had read about people with mental health conditions. I had read stories in newspapers about them stabbing innocent strangers in parks. I was not a freak. Okay, so I felt really uncomfortable living in my skin most of the time. That did not make me a freak. I felt uncomfortable being on my own unless I had something to occupy me. Something that meant I did not have to feel my discomfort. I felt uncomfortable in groups as well. Anything more than just one other person to deal with and I felt uncomfortable. Give me just one person any day. Somebody I know really well or a total stranger. It did not really matter. I loved dealing with just one other person. You can really focus on just one other person. Really get lost in just one other person. Get into their lives. Get into their holidays. Get into their hobbies. Get into their interests. Get into their problems. Get into their skin. Get out of your own. Mental health was not something people really talked about. It was not something I had ever discussed with my just one other persons.

I held this view for a month or so until I calmed down enough to think more appropriately about it. I decided that I should at least do some research into it and keep an open mind for now. This is where the internet was really useful. I sat for hours looking at what was available on reputable sites. After a couple of days, I realised that I did have a lot of the traits associated with being bipolar. After about another week of research, I had come round to accepting that I probably was bipolar. If I was going to be in this box, then I wanted to get something out of it. I now wanted to make sure I was able to identify that another possible episode was coming so that I could seek treatment immediately and hopefully avoid another hospital admission. I identified my triggers and tell-tale signs.

My main triggers were travel (in particular to countries where English is not the first language) and stress and my main tell-tale sign was that I did not need my usual eight hours of sleep. This knowledge proved very useful some years later when the local Council suddenly decided to close the primary school my youngest child was attending. I recognised that my sleep was being disturbed and took myself straight to the doctor. I phoned the receptionist first thing and informed her that I had a serious mental health problem and that I needed to see a specific doctor that morning so that what would very shortly become a serious episode could be averted. To my amazement I was allocated an early appointment slot. I went in and explained my situation, got some appropriate medication and this episode was nipped in the bud. My evenings of research had not been in vain.

I had been put on Lithium during my second episode and would stay on it for a total of nine to ten years. On a visit to the doctor's surgery on a totally different issue, the doctor I was seeing informed me that I needed to consider coming off Lithium. It was not a good idea to stay on it for too long. I must admit I was getting fed up with the regular blood tests but I was very concerned about going high again. The doctor produced a plan of action for me to slowly reduce over six weeks the amount I took. I nervously followed the plan and successfully withdrew.

I was warned that the statistics around my condition indicated that I should expect to have more episodes during my lifetime. I had managed to nip one in the bud already and so I was a little reassured by this but still concerned that I could end up in hospital again.

A Working Mother

A Mental Illness Observed

By way of introduction, I must tell you that I have never met this writer. Philip made contact with me by telephone and by email after reading about me in a newspaper. He very gently told me a little about himself and asked if he might telephone me from time to time to share his thoughts and insights. I had no problem with this. Philip has been in touch for a number of years now. He has always respected the fact that I have a busy life with our family and with pastoral groups, etcetera, and he is very careful not to take up too much of my time. I, on the other hand, have learnt from Philip more of the despair that individuals like him undergo when experiencing severe episodes of depression. So it has been an educational journey for me and hopefully a supportive time for Philip. Had Philip lived nearer to me, I would have welcomed him into our pastoral support group but this was not possible as he lives in a different part of the country.

Philip has battled courageously with his depression over many, many years and has tried on occasions and sometimes successfully to return to work. He has struggled to come to terms with the fact that he will probably always be on medication. He acknowledges that it is unlikely that he will be in paid employment again unless his health drastically improves.

When attending services in his Anglican church, Philip finds it very difficult to communicate with others because of his depression. He is frightened of being a nuisance or a burden and consequently is reluctant to engage in conversation in case others do not want to hear of his struggles with his depression. This leaves him feeling lonely and isolated.

Over the years I have sensed a definite improvement in Philip's outlook and determination to live with his illness and he has found strategies to help him through the more difficult times. He has my admiration and respect for his doggedness in battling on in all weathers.

Philip found putting pen to paper to write about mental illness an extremely hard task and on a number of occasions told me that he was unable to do it, but with great strength of character and with courage, he succeeded and sent me his contribution.

A Mental Illness Observed

It is not a low mood or feeling down but an unbearable emotional state and one that lasts weeks and months. It is quite primitive and involuntary and beyond our normal rational and felt experiences - thoughts speed by fast, attention is hyper vigilant, emotional feelings painful, terrifying and excruciating with bouts of crying. It comes by itself and like an atmospheric storm is turbulent and devastating and only after those weeks and months does calm return. I can only think that the primitive and involuntary parts of the brain (mid brain and brain stem) are over-active at these times and rational thinking is impaired.

Another point to make is the way it undercuts your self or personality, leaving it demoralised and unable to fight back, like say, being at sea and shipwrecked, with nothing to cling on to. Then relations with others are impaired - simply talking becomes difficult - and there is an acute sense of being alone and isolated. Here the sense of agency, of being able to do something about it, is impaired. You become dependent on others for a while until agency returns.

Clinical And Scientific: Helpful Clinical And Psychological Literature

Allen Jon (2006) *Coping with Depression.*
American Psychiatric Publishing Inc, Arlington, VA, USA

Allen is an academic and clinician working in the
Menninger Clinic, in Texas.
He combines understanding with hope and surveys
causes and treatments.

Corveleyn, Luyten, Blatt eds. (2005) *Theories of
Depression.*
Leuven University Press, Leuven, Belgium; Lawrence
Erlbaum Associates, Mahwah, New Jersey, USA

These writers respect both psychoanalytic and cognitive
theories, often separated in clinical practice.   Sidney
Blatt defines self-critical and dependency depression
and posits an interactive model of depression, the
developmental and relational roots of the personality
interacting with psycho-social stresses and negative life
events.

Gilbert Paul ed. (2009) *Compassion.*
Routledge, Hove East, Sussex

Gilbert explores the clinical and psychological value of
compassion, drawing on evolutionary, cognitive and
Buddhist ideas.

Lyubomirsky Sonja (2010) *The How of Happiness.*
Piatkus, an Imprint of Little Brown Group, London

Frederickson Barbara (2011) *Positivity.*
Oneworld Publications, Oxford

Both these are well researched with a positive
psychology approach.

Religion And Faith

Whereas science solves problems, religion is
providential - about our care and protection, through our
prayers, friends and families, doctors, charities and
churches, and as a mentally ill person, is still giving me
back my dignity and reduces my suffering.

'There is nothing abstract about the faith we share... we
know that people will be there for us when we need
them.' Sacks Jonathan (2000) *Celebrating Life.* Fount,
an Imprint of Harper Collins, London

Psalms 71, 86 (1984) *Book of Common Prayer Vol. I.*
Church in Wales Publications, Penarth, Glamorgan

'Set thou me free from all my troubles, O turn thee unto
me and comfort me'

'But thou O Lord art full of compassion and mercy,
Long suffering, plenteous in goodness and truth'

An extract below from an address by John Paul II at a
Conference on Pastoral Care and Depression,
14 November 2003.

'... It is therefore important to stretch out a hand to the sick, to make them perceive the tenderness of God, to integrate them into a community of faith and life in which they can feel accepted, understood, supported, respected; in a word, in which they can love and be loved. For them as for everyone else, contemplating Christ means letting oneself be 'looked at' by Him, an experience that opens one to hope and convinces one to choose life (cf. Dt.30:19).

In the spiritual process, reading and meditation on the Psalms, in which the sacred author expresses his joys and anxieties in prayer, can be of great help. The recitation of the Rosary makes it possible to find in Mary a loving Mother who teaches us how to live in Christ. Participation in the Eucharist is a source of inner peace, because of the effectiveness of the Word and of the Bread of Life, and because of the integration into the ecclesiastical community that it achieves. Aware of the effort it costs a depressed person to do something which to others appears simple and spontaneous, one must endeavour to help him with patience and sensitivity, remembering the observation of St Theresa of the Child Jesus: 'Little ones take little steps'.

In his infinite love, God is always close to those who are suffering. Depressive illness can be a way to discover other aspects of oneself and new forms of encounter with God. Christ listens to the cry of those whose boat is rocked by the storm (cf. Mk.4:35-41). He is present beside them to help them in the crossing and guide them to the harbour of rediscovered peace...'

Philip J

Kaleidoscope

My head is like a kaleidoscope.

Bits and pieces swirling; images and patterns ever
changing;

A maelstrom of feelings, twisting, tossing, turning, going
round and round and round,

And every time the pattern sets, a new thought comes
creeping in.

So the pattern breaks, reforms and tears; bringing back
the lonely years,

Gathering in the memories until coherent thought is lost.

Images flash in and out, a glance, a look, a hand held
out; a pair of flashing eyes.

Snatches, sounds of conversation speak a cacophony
of jumbled voices,

Angry, pleading, loving, joyous, sad and wearily
resigned,

Echoing, tugging, and resounding through my mind.

Was it real or just imagined? Did you feel the way I
thought?

Or was it all illusion by a longing, dearly bought?

Deep, deep down, the memories take me,

Helpless in the torrent of emotion, surging, pulling me all
ways.

I have to move on but which way to turn?

How to calm the current raging through my brain?

I have been this way before and survived.

I did not know the roots of feeling had gone so deep.

Can I pull myself together once more?

Gather parts all torn and splintered yet again?

Find a balance, mesh the pieces; make a whole of
broken dreams?

Again? And again? And again... and again... and
again..........

I do not know... I just don't know.........

May God forgive me, I just don't know.....

Kate

Writer's name has been changed by request

Only A Miracle Will Set Us Free

When Joy came for the first time to our pastoral support meeting for people experiencing mental ill health in our communities, I specifically remember my meeting with her because she was so depressed. I was worried that it might be off-putting for the others in the group. This was not so. I think everyone present had empathy with Joy. When she shared quite openly and honestly, over the months, her suicidal thoughts and her lack of enthusiasm about living, I think the small number of people present easily identified with her. I find her such a lovable, thoughtful and caring person. I yearned for her to relocate with the happy world she once dwelt in.

She shared her progress, her black days and the infrequent lighter moments. She told how over time, her husband and adult children addressed her in different ways, trying to help her out of her blackness. Sometimes it was most painful for her as she felt that they did not really understand how ill she was and how she was unable to help herself. She found her daughter to be a rock for her when she felt so disabled by her condition. She knew her husband was doing his best to be alongside her even though his treatment of her was not always as she would have liked. He cared deeply for her and no doubt was frustrated in his efforts to help her regain good health. Joy grieved at not being able to look after her grandchildren as she used to. She felt she was missing out on so much in her life due to this debilitating illness.

Joy brought her diary one day and read sections to us. When she was very ill, she found she could express her feelings and anguish in poetry and over the years had put down her thoughts in verse. The diary input relates to her depth of despair, especially over the deaths, one by one, of her beloved dogs and of her slide into severe depression. I present the writings below.

April 2005

'The countryside just now is so sublime, lush leaves, lemon, lilac and lime
The loveliness heightens the sadness in me and stirs up thoughts about what has to be
Every living thing will die and fade away and will not see another wondrous day
Gone are our dogs Oscar, Drift and Rhea and the world without them to me is so drear
Their lives were so brief. They left me full of grief
And Axle will soon follow which will swell my sorrow
It seems such a waste, in such bad taste
That these beautiful creatures in both nature and features are gone! Are none!
Maybe in another time and place I will see again each lovely face
Oh what a meeting, what a tail wagging greeting
United again with father and brother, friends, neighbours, grandpops and grandmothers
All these who departed before who made my life worth living for
How miraculous to be with them all again without old age and without their final pain
It all seems too good to be true and leaves me feeling so, so blue
If there is nothing more, then what has it all been for?'

July 2005

'June and July have seen me so low, so low in fact I've wanted to go
Bereft of any joy in life, full of sickening, sickly strife
But through it all stood Andrea my daughter, more sustenance to me than food and water

Her beside me has meant so much, reassured by her loving touch

I'm so proud of what she's become, caring nurse, wonderful mum

She truly is a very great treasure, so great that it is surely without measure

And what about child number one, strong and hardy, Lee, my son

He says no wonder I'm full of gloom sitting day after day in the same old room

He's come up with his unique plot to get me out each day be it cold or hot

So I'm hoping August and September will give me cheerier days to remember

If they do, I'll know who to thank, my steadfast children on whom I can bank

Darren and Kendra, my son and daughter-in-law could not really have done any more

To be patient and kind and show that they care; if I needed them I knew they'd be there

And I've discovered I have many a good friend who took the time to make sure I was on the mend

Anne R, Margaret, Kath, Anne G, Pat and Sue showed care, consideration and gave of their time too

My husband's been by my side every hour even though I make his life dour

He's waited on me hand and foot trying to get me out of this rut

So come on Joy, make an effort to get well and lift me and all out of this hell!'

Autumn 2005

'In September the news I was given was that sweet, nervous Tarka was no longer living

She was one dog amongst a lot and never got as much love and attention as the older dogs got

I've been ill for ever so long, so I never got the chance to right that wrong
That made me feel sad and ever so bad
In October there was more heartbreak, these losses were getting too hard to take
My mother announced, 'Axle has died'; my heart broke, my soul bitterly cried
Never again to see that beautiful gentle face; no-one or no other could take his place
The time we shared was happy and glad; I'll never forget the wonderful time we had
I hope all their days are safe and pain free and looking forward to the day they'll see me!'

December 2006

'I am ill, still; I wish there was a pill
To put me right by tomorrow night
My life has been taken, my mind is all shaken
Give me back my life, take away this strife
So I can feel good like every human being should!'

July 2007

'Why are living things here on earth? It's unclear what is the purpose or worth
Our brains are programmed to value life and yet life is punctuated with pain and strife
To die is the worst thing a living thing will do and yet we know it will happen to me and you
It's senseless for living things to 'be'; the reason for it I just cannot see
I'm finding life mundane and mirthless; each day becomes more and more worthless
I would like my life to be willingly given to someone losing theirs but longing to go on living
My joy in life has gone very bad; all I can feel is useless and sad

Shouldn't we all make a firm resolve to make this illogical world devolve!

Let everything living stop reproducing; then life on Earth will begin reducing

And so will illness, suffering and pain never to raise its ugly head again

All that will be left is gas, liquid and solid; that idea to me is far from horrid

I wish it had happened in a previous dawn so that I need never have been created and born

But the day will come when I go to sleep which will be everlasting and so very deep

I will then be unthinking and my brain so numb; I am not sorry that that day will come

I will be free because there will be no me

I can't bear to think there's another day tomorrow, a time to pretend well-being, instead of showing sorrow

If I could transplant my life into Brian my brother; what a glorious gift for him and his mother

His love of life was true and firm. The thought of going on like this makes me squirm

To end it will cause my loved ones pain but their loss would be my gain

I cannot keep living this pointless futile existence; between it and me there needs to be distance

Then Allan could start to live a better life instead of being burdened by a useless wife!

I don't think I've seen for quite a while Allan's face brighten with a cheerful smile

And it's all because of worthless me; no wonder I don't really want to 'be'

When I'm very depressed, his loving flies away; it's then I feel most I don't want to stay

Everyone at first I'm sure will grieve but pretty soon that feeling will up and leave

And they will get on with their days good and bad, living illogically but feeling mostly glad'

August 2007

'I need to stop kidding myself. My life is over; I'm just on a shelf
I sit there gathering cobwebs and dust, parts of me have already turned into rust
I'll never find the original me; this is how I will permanently be
Unable to join in the mainstream of life bringing no-one joy, only strife
Everyone seems to know where they're going, for me there simply is no knowing
I am lost, I have no goal; I feel as if I'm in a black hole
I cannot shop, I cannot cook; I get no joy from reading a book
I can't garden; I can't go for a hike. It's impossible for me to ride a bike
I can't paddle or go for a swim. Life is dull and pretty grim
I'd love to give my grandchildren time; play games with them, teach them a rhyme
There is nothing much I can do, just feeling purposeless and ever so blue
I wish I could go to sleep and not wake. It would be better for everyone's sake
There are many places I would love to see but I'm afraid that's not for me
The scenes that used to make my spirit soar do not have that effect any more
It all looks transient and forlorn; it won't exist in some future dawn
I worry about what will be tomorrow; happiness will flee to be replaced by sorrow
My husband cannot understand my depression; it fills him with anger and aggression
His eyes bulge and his pulses race when all I want is a tender embrace

But this has gone on far too long and I know that I am in the wrong
It's all my fault that things are bad; I'm never happy, always sad
Everyone is tired of me. I need to be how I used to be
All my time needs to come to an end before I send good people round the bend'

October 2007

'I no longer want to live; I have nothing left to give
I can't take care of myself; I need putting on a shelf
But then I'd be a waste of space; I have no saving grace
My son is always sad; he thinks his life is bad
I don't know what to do; it makes me feel more blue
My life just has no point; I'm feeling all out of joint
I'm tired of it all; my back's against the wall
I've tried to do my best; now I just want eternal rest
It will set my husband free; he won't have to see me
I've lost my love of life; there seems to be nothing but strife
I've lost all hope, I just can't cope
My sadness is heaping, I can't stop weeping
I'm beaten and crushed, my optimism mushed
This all must cease; I need some peace
I want my spirit to soar; I can't take any more'

December 2009

'Just what am I going to do? I'm full of angst and so deeply blue
I've managed to cease taking anti-depressant pills but that has not rid me of all ills
It's brought me down into a pit of despair; I've tried so hard my health to repair
But here I lie in my lonely bed believing that I'd be better off dead

How long can this torture go on? I felt so sure by now it would be gone
I feel inside me a desperate need to make me well with God I plead
He either doesn't hear or doesn't care about my need
I don't want all the things that only money can buy; I just want to smile and not to cry
To peacefully walk and see the beauty around; to run with my grandchildren and hear my heart pound
To sleep a whole night through; to wake happy and fresh and greet the day anew
Instead I wake absolutely worn out; it takes me ages to get out about
Out and about? I mean down the stairs to spend another day full of anxiety and cares
I'm making my husband as ill as me; in another year's time where will we be?
Our future seems to hold no hope; both of us are finding we cannot cope
Only a miracle will set us free and that happening I just cannot see!'

Recap

Joy briefly related to us how it all began and why she eventually sought out our pastoral support group.

'The first sign that something was not right was pulsating muscles all over my body; then extreme fatigue and eventually a feeling of severe anxiety. I was unable to sleep but if I managed to drop off, I would be woken quite soon with dreadful dreams. Most of the night was spent walking from room to room, or around the garden, punctuated by attempts to go to sleep.

I was treated with anti-depressants that were changed about four times. Nothing seemed to help. I eventually phoned my GP's surgery and cried down the phone, 'somebody help me!' The doctor came and I went into a mental hospital for three weeks, but after being discharged, I was still very little better.

I saw a psychiatrist every month or so and the anti-depressants I was prescribed were changed again. I improved somewhat but was desperate for a spiritual uplift similar to the feelings I had when I was walking on wide, open moors or through woodland with shafts of light coming through the trees and birds singing. I did not want visitors, not even my mother or my daughter, and so I lost touch with my grandchildren, which saddened me even more.

My mother's friend heard Edna talk on the local radio and told my mother that Edna could perhaps help me. I contacted her and plucked up courage to come to this group. It was the first time I was able to tell of my illogical feelings and knew you would understand and not judge. It was good meeting Father Bill when he attended and whom I know helped initiate the group and I found him a great source of understanding and wisdom.'

Joy continues her story by relating her gentle improvement in health.
'I gradually started to gain confidence enough to go to study groups in the Catholic Church, and also to Taize evenings which were a great source of peace and spiritual uplift. One service that I attended told us the story of the sick lady who could not reach Jesus to ask him for a cure. She managed to push through crowds and touch his robe and was cured. The priest in the church put his robe around the Eucharist and invited us to come and touch it and ask God for what we needed. It was a transforming moment and I felt I had found myself again. This lasted for three days, but the horrible anxiety returned.

I continue to go to special church activities and to Edna's group. I am slowly improving and can go to social events, visit friends, spend time with my grandchildren, and invite friends to my house. I will continue to use the Catholic Church, which is really the people belonging to it, and I know that, along with attending Edna's group, I will eventually get well enough to be glad I am alive.'

Signs Of Restoration

Little by little, we could see that Joy was improving. The participants in the group listened with empathy and affirmed her small measures of success. Week by week, it is not easy to notice the minute signs of restoration of good health oneself, but members were able to point out indications of hope to her.

Joy surprised us all one day by arriving on a mobility scooter. Up to this point, her husband had been bringing her to the meetings and picking her up. This was truly a step forward as it allowed Joy the freedom to enjoy the open air, the sunshine, the green trees and scenery around her home. She always loved to walk in the countryside and this was a taste of better things to come. Her husband continued to bring Joy when the weather was not good enough for her to be in the open air but when the weather was kind she continued to take herself out on her scooter.

Slowly we began to see Joy climb out of her depression and have a more positive hopeful vision for the future. Although she is a long way from being back to good health, the improvements are obvious to those around her and her attitude and endeavours to regain better health are a source of admiration for us all.

The rain was pouring down this week when our meeting was due to take place. The telephone rang and I picked up the receiver.

'Hello.'

'Hello, Edna. It's Joy. Are you coming to the meeting this afternoon?'

'Hello, Joy. Good to hear from you and yes, I am going to the meeting.'

'Would you like me to pick you up?'

'That would be great, Joy. Thank you.'

'I'll see you at ten to one then.'

'Okay. Thank you. See you then. Bye.' I came off the phone and only then realised that Joy must be driving again. This is good news and another small step on the way to recovery and a brighter future. When Joy picked me up, I commented on this and she said that she only drove short distances around her home but it was a start.

'I am still getting a bit mixed up with the indicator switch and window wipers but I am getting there.'

'Joy, I think it is brilliant.' I reflected when I returned home on Joy's journey and her many struggles and changes of medications and her deep longings to get better. She has laboured on in pain and distress and severe anxiety but her resilience has played a part in her slowly coming to a better place. There is a light for her now, I feel, and hope for the future.

When I gave this write-up to Joy to proof read she returned it with the comment, 'Just a couple of typing errors!' Then she added, 'It was novel reading those poems again - it brought home to me just how much better I am. Thank you for all the help the (pastoral) group has given me over the years. I had forgotten how unhappy I was with my life! I am in a much better place now.'

Joy McInnes

Message of Hope

As an introduction to this contributor, I would like to tell you how we came to communicate with one another even though we have never met. Ken wrote me a letter after reading of my published books in *Being Alongside*, a bi-monthly newsletter. *Being Alongside* is the operating name of the *Association of Pastoral Care in Mental Health - Being Alongside*, a Christian-based voluntary association of individual members and affiliated groups who recognise the importance of spiritual values and support in mental health.

Having discovered that I had managed to get my works published, Ken, who has written many articles and pamphlets over the years, wanted to know if I could help him get his biography published. I was able to help him through contacts I had and *An Adventurous Life* by Pastor Ken Bunting RMN (2010, Fryup Press, Whitby), was published. We corresponded on numerous occasions whilst this task was being fulfilled. Ken does not use a computer. He types everything on an old typewriter and then it has to be transferred to a computer by another. So the whole process was time consuming but very rewarding on all sides.

Amongst the many titles of Ken's pamphlets and publications is: *Ignoring the Divine Psychiatrist*. Ken describes this particular writing thus: 'Almost a lifetime in the psychiatric profession, with both 'hands on' and managerial experience, has long convinced me, the author, that even a 'grain of mustard seed' faith in God will help the sufferer towards improvement and recovery, rather than merely trying by his or her own unaided resources.'

I must add now that when Ken introduced himself to me, he and his wife Beryl were already in their eighties, in failing health and in sheltered accommodation. As I typed up his biography onto my computer, I became more and more impressed with his life of ministry and service, particularly to those experiencing mental ill health. Ken was not always a Christian, but told me that having found Jesus Christ, he and his wife lived out their lives in dedication to helping others less fortunate than themselves and are still living out these Gospel values in spite of their advanced years.

In his earlier life, Ken became part of the Fellowship Movement. I am a Roman Catholic, but as Ken pointed out, although we differ a little in our religious persuasions, mental illness does not know denominational divisions. It is what we have in common in wanting to help people with mental ill health and in demonstrating the importance of a holistic approach including spiritual nourishment that is important.

Ken's earnest belief is that that which is generally called 'mental illness' is often worsened by the hostile and unfriendly attitude of the prevailing environment. Over his thirty-five years in the psychiatric profession, he has proved many, many times that a kind befriending atmosphere helps many on the path of restoration. He has held the view for many years that Jesus for 'traditional religion' often obscures the need for followers of Christ to give help to needy and underprivileged people. Ken's long-held conviction, through his service and activities as a psychiatric nurse, is that to hold a strong faith in God is the only proved and practical way to take steps in the direction of improvement towards recovery.

Not only does Ken hold this conviction, but through a life dedicated to preaching, praying, listening, writing books, giving seminars, producing tapes and videos, and unremitting correspondence, he can demonstrate the truth of his convictions through the hundreds of letters he has received from the scores of individuals who have been helped towards restoration by his message of hope. He maintains that one does not need to be highly qualified or an ordained minister or priest in order to 'Be Alongside' persons with mental illnesses. Ken is not only a man of words but has also put his faith into action (Jm.2:18), an example to us all of living one's life for others, as has his wife Beryl, both grounded in their belief in Jesus Christ and in the words of the Gospel that:

In truth I tell you, in so far as you did this to one of the least of these brothers (and sisters) of mine, you did it to Me (Mt.25:40)

When I told Ken of my third book and invited him to send a contribution, he sent not one poem but two

.

Where Would I Be?
(inspired by Edna's books)

Where would I be had you not come and sat along
beside me?
And listened to my jumbled words which like a raging
sea
Had torn apart my muddled mind filled with despair and
dread
And made me wish that I was dead
And though you said but little - only wait until my tirade
Like a river in its spate would cause well-meaning ones
to tire and go
And leave me all alone to face my woe
Yet you have shown me truly Christian love of Jesus
who went about just doing good
We long that those, who say they 'have His mind'
Would be as He was, loving, patient, kind

A Carer's Lament

I've cared for the Youngsters, the Old and Infirm
I've nurtured the Ones with no prospects to learn
I've spent many years with those Mentally Ill
I've memories of these, which none other can fill
I've spent sleepless nights tending Dying and Sick
I've cared for the Troubled until mentally fit
Like Jesus, whose once-darkened souls He has lit
And now I am old and as tired as can be
I wonder who's going to look after me
Thank God, we've a Saviour who says he will not
For a moment forsake us whatever our lot!

Pastor Ken Bunting RMN

Edna Hunneysett

Send Forth Your Spirit

There are people close to us
Perhaps they are feeling overwhelmed by loneliness
and despair
Perhaps we are overwhelmed by the despair they feel

Help us Lord to bring our healing to them
Bond us through what is holy and sacred

Help us to journey with them through ourselves and our
parish community
Help us to share their pain and uncertainties
Let the gift of understanding flow through us

Help them to experience your love and healing
Let our meeting be an encounter
Where the power of your grace is present

Send forth your Spirit
To inspire and nurture all those who experience mental
distress

We ask this in your name's sake

Amen

Ben

Our Lady of Mental Peace

This information was sent to me some years ago by Margaret when she lived in the United Kingdom. She had invited me to speak at a Conference that she had organised in May 2003 and it was there that I learned from Margaret of the devotion to Our Lady of Mental Peace. Margaret has since emigrated. She asked me at the time if I would promote this devotion in England. I try to do this wherever I go to raise awareness of support needed for those with mental illnesses and their families, especially when I speak at Masses or at Conferences, and I take the prayer cards with me to distribute to anyone wanting one.

Margaret tells her story by firstly quoting a prayer taken from the prayer card:

Mother of tranquillity, Mother of hope, Our Lady of Mental Peace, we reach out to you for what is needful in our weakness. Teach a searching heart that God's love is unchanging. That human love begins and grows by touching His Love.
Our Lady of Mental Peace, pray for us.

'This, the very prayer we shared in the first few meetings of our mental health support group, set up in August 2000. Clearly, not knowing where this may lead, we agreed to adopt Our Lady as our patron, giving her this new title, Our Lady of Mental Peace.

Several weeks on, Bob, one of our members, arrived at the group, excitedly drawing from his pocket a small purse belonging to his wife Maisie. Inside, a medal of Our Lady of Mental Peace and a prayer card, our prayer clearly printed, among others. A contact address too for further information: Catholic Chaplain's Office,

Metropolitan State Hospital, Waltham, Massachusetts. I was curious. I wrote off to the State Hospital. A time after, when all seemed lost, I was introduced to the wonders of the internet, searching for Waltham, Massachusetts, and it even gave me a street map. I looked up Catholic churches, took the addresses and sent off to various parish priests.

Eventually a Father Bill Leonard of the Archdiocese of Boston confirmed that the hospital had indeed closed in 1992. He had been chaplain there in its last three years. He was able to share that the devotion to Our Lady of Mental Peace was a private devotion. The medal had been a graceful design of a Notre Dame nun, Sister St Vincent de Paul, and a Catholic Mental Hospital chaplain and blessed by both Pope John XXIII and Pope Paul VI. A twelve foot statue of Our Lady of Mental Peace was dedicated on May 23rd 1963 by Richard Cardinal Cushing at the Metropolitan State Hospital and mounted on the outside wall. Cardinal Cushing was a great supporter of persons with mental illnesses, building chapels within three of the state psychiatric hospitals in the Archdiocese of Boston. A quote by Richard Cardinal Cushing Archbishop of Boston taken from the prayer card:

I am sure that if Christ and his Blessed Mother were on earth today, they would spend much of their time among those mentally ill

Father Leonard gave a further contact, an elderly Monsignor William Sullivan. Monsignor Sullivan spent twenty-seven years as a chaplain working in Massachusetts with people who were mentally ill. I was soon to discover that he was indeed the founder of the devotion, founding this new title, Our Lady of Mental Peace, in 1954. He had been chaplain at the Metropolitan State Hospital from 1958 to 1968. He was able to go back a little further than Father Leonard with the information that the first chaplains decided to promote the proper place of Mary in mental health by introducing a weekly rosary programme, in the hospital's thirty wards, way back in 1956. Continuing the emphasis on the place of Mary in their lives, the Legion of Mary was asked to set up a presidium at the hospital... and so Mary was given her place. Both programmes were very much a part of hospital life. The Monsignor spent thirty years as a psychiatric hospital chaplain working in Massachusetts, assisted by the Legion of Mary, and was encouraged to develop the devotion by Cardinal Cushing. The Legion of Mary was invited to set up a presidium at the different hospitals. The rosary was regularly recited throughout the wards...

The patients feel that this new title for Mary will make mental ill health her specific concern, and they place more confidence in it than in any other devotion.

It is this devotion that we would like to promote in the United Kingdom, and beyond... We began by celebrating a Mass in her honour. Medals and prayer cards were made available. It was an overwhelming success. We are promoting too, the setting up of two mental health support groups in our area, with Our Lady of Mental Peace as our patron. As a Catholic support group, time is given for prayer and reflection in addition to information giving and mutual support. Since the inaugural Mass, the media has picked up the story behind the devotion. It is a story, indeed a devotion, that is now worldwide, a devotion to share with your family and friends.

In the meantime I continue to keep in touch with Monsignor William Sullivan. He tells me that our sponsoring the devotion to Our Lady of Mental Peace is the only active group known to be doing so. He has forwarded to me all remaining medals and prayer cards in the hope that we may continue to support and promote this devotion. Given such an honour, I feel it is important for us to continue his life's work. A closing prayer by Monsignor William Sullivan taken from the prayer card:

Eternal God, teach us the knowledge and the skills that we need for the problem of mental health. But because neither knowledge nor skills will ever get us to properly know ourselves or anyone else, for only love does this, teach us first to love...

In July 2003, some two years after establishing two mental health support groups here in the United Kingdom, I made arrangements to meet Monsignor Sullivan in his home town of Boston. We had stumbled upon the title of Our Lady of Mental Peace by sheer providence and I had been corresponding with the Monsignor since October 2000. He arrived in the hotel foyer, leaning over his walking stick, wearing a radiant smile. We sat talking over lunch; then one coffee after another. We discussed many different aspects to the devotion and how we might continue to encourage it among the laity. Whilst it is a private devotion, Monsignor Sullivan has agreed to our adopting Our Lady of Mental Peace as a patron of support groups. As users and carers of mental health services, we can assist others by sharing our experiences and learning from them. We organise various activities too and more importantly, we pray together. Monsignor Sullivan was very conscious of the stigma conjured up when addressing mental health issues. Meeting him was in deed a blessing. He is a very inspirational and caring man. Fortunately I was able to make a further visit to Monsignor Sullivan shortly before he died in July, 2006.

The devotion is presently active in many parts of the United Kingdom, among the Religious and the Laity. The devotion is also active in Perth, Western Australia, and in Hamilton, New Zealand. This devotion to Our Lady is for everyone, not only for a person experiencing a mental illness, as we all have a measure of mental well-being. Often there is an imbalance in our lives no matter how careful we are. We all need mental peace in our lives. We trust that this devotion will be allowed to flourish and be a source of comfort and support to those in need.'

Margaret

Prayer cards obtainable from Mackay & Inglis Ltd, Printers, 19, Polmadie Street, Glasgow G42 0PG

Some names have been changed by request

Our Suicidal Children: Where are you God?
(2009) Chipmunkapublishing

About the Book

This book is the story of an ordinary mother's personal family life through the nightmare of caring for a teenage daughter with acute clinical depression. With no previous training, the author has built on her experiences as a carer and examines the difficulties posed to people, including those with a Christian faith. Beyond the personal dimension, the author examines support given to carers and specifically that given by the Catholic Church. She produces stirring evidence in support of her view that more needs to be done to help this vulnerable group. The book will provide valuable information to many carers who feel isolated and unsupported. It will also be of considerable interest to the professionals who offer help in such circumstances. In attempting to identify the particular benefit and importance of the dimension of spiritual support, it also provides a valuable reference for the Churches.

Reviews

What does it mean to care and be cared for? This is the theological and practical question that lies at the heart of this book. In wrestling her way towards an answer, Edna Hunneysett provides us with an invaluable and deeply moving insight into what it means to care for a person with a severe mental illness, and the sometimes intolerable strains that such a task places on family and carers. The book provides us with fresh challenges and insights that should enable us all to care a bit more deeply and to understand the inner world of carer and cared for a bit more compassionately. In telling the story of her experiences as a carer, Hunneysett insightfully highlights the inadequacies of the Church's response to both carers and cared for, and lays down some vital challenges which call the Church to take very seriously its ministry to people with mental health problems and their families. This is more than a book about mental illness. It is about being human and enabling others to remain human even in the midst of the most formidable storms. Everyone who has an interest in caring for people with mental illnesses and ensuring that carers are cared for should take seriously the insights and challenges presented in this book.

Rev. Professor John Swinton
Professor in Practical Theology and Pastoral Care
King's College University of Aberdeen

A very personal family story that will strike a chord with very many readers.

Very Rev. Canon Edmond Gubbins
Diocese of Middlesbrough

An excellent book in which the author demonstrates that the gap between the spiritual and the secular in the world of healing can be bridged.

Dr Danny T Donovan

Those with mental health difficulties and their carers look to Christian communities for understanding and support. Edna Hunneysett's searingly honest and poignant work helps us recognise our responsibilities and rise to the challenges... A marvellously clear summons, arising from lived experiences...

Rt Rev. Professor Stephen Sykes
Formerly Bishop of Ely and retired Principal of St. John's
College, Durham

Edna Hunneysett

Pastoral Care Mental Health
(2009) Chipmunkapublishing

About the Book / Reviews

The story behind this book is truly remarkable. The author, a sixty-eight year old Catholic mother with eight children and sixteen grandchildren, began her tertiary education at the age of fifty. It was when her thirteen-year-old daughter fell into a severe clinical depression that she began to experience for herself the limitations of her Church's capacity to cope with people with mental illnesses and their families. From then onwards she has devoted herself to studying, writing and speaking about the phenomena and prejudice, stigma and discrimination within Christian congregations.

This is the second work she has written. The first, *Our Suicidal Teenagers: Where are you God?* included a study of attitudes gleaned from four Catholic clergy on the pastoral care of sick people, including those with mental illnesses. The present work, which is an entirely new enterprise, extends the range of her enquiry to congregations in three different ecclesiastical traditions, Catholic, Anglican and Evangelical/Pentecostal. She is looking for answers to such questions as: Is there care in Christian communities towards people with mental illnesses? Do Christians know what kind of support people with mental illnesses and their families need? Does the Christian faith make a difference to how such people are treated? Are Christian priests trained in this aspect of ministry?

But first, Hunneysett gives us an account, gleaned from her wide reading, of the historical development of the Christian theological understanding of insanity, from the New Testament times onwards. The story turns, of course, upon the eighteenth century enlightenment and the widespread but not universal abandonment of demon possession as an explanation. Psychiatry as a profession originates in the nineteenth century, and the building of asylums for insane people led to hopes that cures would be found. As Hunneysett makes clear, the dissolution of the monasteries had resulted in the closure of places offering shelter to old, sick and incapacitated people, among whom persons with mental illnesses were included. At the same time, the understanding that human beings were set apart from animals by the faculty of reason (Aquinas) could give rise to the view that those deprived of their reason were no better than animals. Against this mixed background, Hunneysett devotes an entire chapter to recount Christian developments (of the last two decades) and to growth of local Christian initiatives. But she cautions that 'it is difficult to discern how far this awareness raising, campaigning and support, penetrates the faith communities at grass roots level.'

The book describes the results of questionnaires distributed in the North East of England to three denominations, Anglicans, Roman Catholics and Pentecostal/Evangelical Fellowships. The results are based on a return of nearly forty percent representing some five hundred and ninety-two questionnaires in all. The conclusions of this important and fascinating piece of work are of considerable importance. Whilst it is true that Christian congregations are more accepting of people with mental illnesses than the general public, there is evidence that they are held back by lack of knowledge and the need for better education at every level. There is a real need to raise awareness, so that the negative aspects of mental health difficulties can be addressed, and the stigmatization and discrimination prevalent in society can be challenged. The opportunities which congregations have for raising awareness of the situation of people with mental illnesses and their carers are underlined.

This book shows how it is within the Church's power to make a positive difference to the lives of people with mental health difficulties, written by someone who has made a difference. Hunneysett's is a voice that the Churches must heed.

Rt Rev. Professor Stephen Sykes
Formerly Bishop of Ely and retired Principal of St. John's
College, Durham

This is one of the most in depth studies into the Christian community's response to people with mental health problems that I have come across. Edna, once again, following her previous book, *Our Suicidal Teenagers: Where are you God?* approaches the subject with a wonderful personal touch.

Although this is an incredible piece of research into our, that is, the Christian community's attitudes throughout history and especially in the modern day towards people suffering from mental illness, it is also a deeply personal drawing together of people's lived experience.

Everyone can learn a great deal from this book, as many attitudes commonplace in the Christian community also exist in the wider community. Edna challenges us all to re-evaluate our perception of mental illness and people who suffer from it. These people often feel ignored and misunderstood. The consequences of 'stigma' and negative attitudes towards people who suffer from mental illness are laid bare.

As a chaplain to a hospital specialising in the care of people suffering from mental illnesses and a priest with frequent contact with people affected by mental illnesses, I found this book incredibly thought provoking and I learnt a great deal about my own attitudes, some of which left much to be desired.

For any Christian this is not a comfortable read, patting the Christian Churches on the back for a job well done. It is rather a prophetic call to all Christians and indeed to all people to rise to the summons of Christ to bring 'Good News' to all people; to break down the stereotypes and the stigma that stereotyping brings; and to see all people as children of God and give them the respect that that position deserves. This book is a challenge to Churches and all our attitudes towards mental illness. Edna offers realistic and positive actions for us to take.

Rev. Bill Serplus
Hospital Chaplain, Diocese of Middlesbrough

This book is the fruit of countless hours and days, months of work and thorough research arising out of a lived experience. It will prove to be a source of help and reference and encouragement to many people in the Church and elsewhere in the field of mental health.

Very Rev. Canon Edmond Gubbins
Diocese of Middlesbrough

Lightning Source UK Ltd.
Milton Keynes UK
UKHW011816160419
341127UK00001B/1/P

9 781849 916967